WINE

7,000 BC onwards (all flavours)

Acknowledgement

With thanks to Cath Harries for her original photography which has added sparkle to the book.

First published in November 2015

A catalogue record for this book is available from the British Library

ISBN 978 0 85733 804 4

Library of Congress control no. 2014957389

Published by Haynes Publishing,
Sparkford, Yeovil,
Somerset BA22 7JJ, UK.
Tel: 01963 442030
Int. tel: +44 1963 442030
Website: www.haynes.co.uk

Haynes North America Inc.,
861 Lawrence Drive, Newbury Park,
California 91320, USA.

Printed in the USA by Odcombe Press LP,
1299 Bridgestone Parkway, La Vergne, TN 37086.

Front cover photography: *Cath Harries*

WINE

7,000 BC onwards (all flavours)

Enthusiasts' Manual

A practical guide to the history, appreciation and making of wine

Tim Hampson

CONTENTS

INTRODUCTION

Wine has a cultured history which flows from our prehistoric beginnings to the current day. And it is a little bit of that story we try to tell here.

Within these pages you will find something on the history of wine and its close links with our culture. There are descriptions of how to make wine, be it in a commercial winery or at home.

We explore wine in all its colours and styles and find out what a marvellous companion it is, not just to food but as an ingredient in its own right.

Almost since the first sip of wine was taken it has inspired philosophers, painters, poets, potters and even politicians.

It is a drink of great complexity, which can soar with rich flavours and wonderful aromas. Wine is the drink for kings and queens and it flows like a river through many of our religions. But wine is also the drink of ordinary people, an easy-going drink often made from fruits foraged in the field.

The Egyptians, Greeks and Romans took grapevines with them wherever they went – where their cultures touched can be found traces of winemaking and its consumption.

And so too, when Europeans set off in frail ships to explore the earth and landed in Australia and South and North America, they carried vines. Wine clearly was seen as part of a civilising and civilised life.

It is a drink now made on most continents and in many countries.

In researching this book I was often asked: what is the best wine in the world? What is the best wine you have ever drunk?

I've been lucky and visited some of the finest winemakers on the planet and sipped some of the world's most expensive grand cru wines, destined to be drunk at a fine banquet or dinner.

I've also drunk fresh wine, straight from the barrel, which the maker is proud to call 'vin ordinaire' and say 'this is not for storing, it is for drinking.'

Great wines are all about the moment, the company and the conversation.

Recently on a trip to France, I was in the company of one of France's new wave of innovative winemakers, Domaine Bellevue's Jean-Francois Boras. We decided that we should find a café to eat in.

It was a Monday night, in Cadillac, set in the heart of one of France's great winegrowing areas, Bordeaux. It is a town which England's Henry III revered, because of the wine made here. However, we only found one café open – an Italian pizzeria. A style of café surprisingly common in south-west France.

So as we snacked on slices of freshly made pizza, Jean-Francois ordered a bottle of wine.

Outside the heat of the day still filled the air, it must have been nearly 30°C, and as the sun set and church bells tolled, the day seemed to get no cooler.

In the region of France which produces some of the greatest wines ever made, Jean-Francois ordered a bottle of Italian 8% red Lambrusco. He also asked for some ice cubes.

And so we sat, sipping on our glasses of sparkling red wine, into which we'd put some of the ice cubes. For that moment, it was the perfect wine. Light and refreshing, it lifted our spirits, took some of the heat out of the day and inspired our conversation.

And as the sky went dark and we could clearly see the planets Venus and Jupiter basking in a celestial embrace, I realised, for that moment, I had found the perfect wine.

'Wine' says Jean-Francois, 'enables us to discover who we are.'

This book cannot replicate the tastes and textures of a glass of wine, it cannot repeat the sheer pleasure of drinking a glass of wine and it cannot explore every nuance and fact about the thousands of vineyards and winemakers worldwide.

But this book might just help you find your own perfect moment.

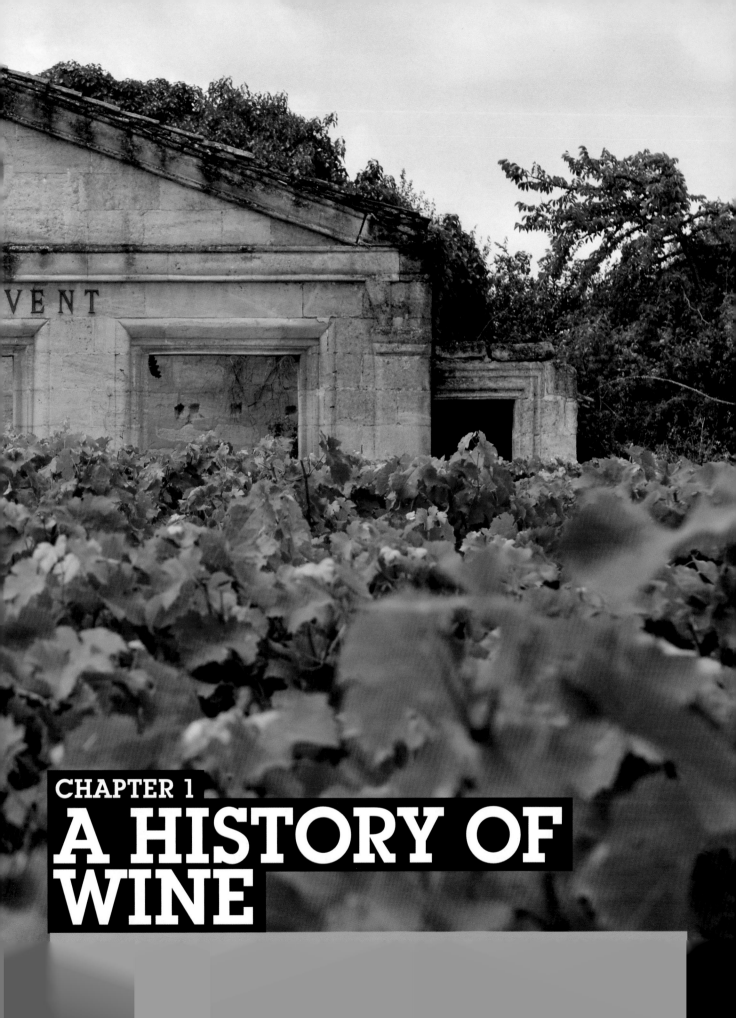

CHAPTER 1
A HISTORY OF WINE

Aged to perfection

So when did people start to make and drink wine? We just don't know.

Wine is certainly as old as civilised time, and plenty of people believe it is indeed much older.

We do know that the creation of alcohol is a natural process and it is thought that all manner of animals, including our ancestors, and birds and insects, enjoyed fermented berries and fruit.

And there is plenty of evidence to show that some 9,000 years ago, either in China or in the sweeping crescent-shaped plains of Mesopotamia, a wine-like drink was made.

Wine isn't quite as old as the hills, but it seems highly likely that in Palaeolithic times, which lasted for almost two million years until about 12,000 years ago, wandering hunter gatherers would have foraged wild grapes growing on vines amongst trees.

Certainly wild grape pips have been found in some pretty ancient settings including the Franchthi Cave in south-east Greece. Occupied for more than 25,000 years it contains evidence of many animals, people and plants, including grape pips from some 12,000 years ago. Though how the grapes were used we do not as yet know.

Another site of grape importance is Balma de l'Abeurador in France. Here in a cave 50 kilometres inland from the Mediterranean Sea on the southern edge of the Massif Central were found the carbonised remains of grapes and other seeds, which may have been domesticated.

Were the grapes sweet and nutritious when ripe? Probably. Did they make a fermented drink from them? Possibly. As

◀ **From the earliest times, people have enjoyed the pleasures of wine.** (Bibliotheque Municipale de Dijon)

grape skins are naturally hosts to yeast spores, it does not need much in the way of a leap of imagination to see how these early humans could first by chance and then by design made a mushy, pulpy drink which contained alcohol.

Winemaking must have been seen as a magical process and its creation one of the first steps for humans on the long road of civilisation.

Professor Patrick McGovern from the Pennsylvania Museum in Philadelphia is known as 'the Indiana Jones of ancient ales, wines, and extreme beverages'. He and his colleagues have found some of the earliest examples of wine in a pottery jar from a Neolithic village in Iran's northern Zagros Mountains. The jar was made sometime between 5400 and 5000 BC.

Who knows, perhaps this drink with its psychotropic powers was enjoyed as people developed the earliest works of art and developed religious and spiritual behaviour. Perhaps one day a biomolecular archaeologist will find evidence of winemaking by Palaeolithic people deep in a cave underground.

Archaeologists have found traces of an alcoholic drink being made about 9,000 years ago in China. Some years ago scientists found traces of grapes mixed with fermented rice and honey on shards of pottery. Certainly many varieties of wild grape were growing in the area at this time.

And certainly many eminent archaeologists are working in the fertile plains of Mesopotamia – now part of Syria and Turkey – searching for ancient wild grapes or evidence of the ancients making wines. For this part of the world is the place where nomadic hunter gatherers first started to domesticate, grow and harvest grains and the academics are looking for evidence that grapes were grown as the foragers became farmers.

Perhaps 2,000 metres high on the top of Nemrut Dagi, in south-eastern Turkey, among the many large stone statues of ancient gods will be found organic evidence of Neolithic winemaking. The scientists search for tartaric acid, a compound which is closely associated with the use of grapes as it is present in ripe grapes and plays a vital part in the maturing of wines.

At one site in northern Israel a 3,700-year-old palatial cellar packed with jars once filled with a wine-like drink has been found. Along with traces of grapes there is evidence of juniper berries, honey, cedar oil and tree resin.

Throughout the ancient world there is evidence on tablets, on papyrus and in tombs that wine was made and enjoyed.

Certainly, history tells us that ancient Egyptians and Mesopotamians planted grapevines and made wine, and there is plenty of evidence to show that wine was an important part of the daily life of the elite and the gods. In the British Museum can be seen a pottery wine jar with a mud seal which dates

siphons used in the year 1450 B.C.

▲ **In ancient times, wine was often not made for people to drink, but for the gods.** (Tour Egypt)

backs to the first dynasty in Egypt in 2950 BC. Not intended for human consumption, it was a drink for the gods.

A modern winemaker would feel at home in an ancient Egyptian vineyard. Many scenes from tombs show how vines were grown and wine made. The best sites were on a hill and if there wasn't a hill then one would be built. To protect the vines a wall would often be put around the plot. Wooden pillars and other types of trellis work would be built and pruning was commonplace to keep the growth of the vines low. The shape of the support forms a hieroglyph which is used in the words meaning 'garden', 'wine', and 'vine'.

When the grapes were ripe they were picked and put into large rush baskets. The grapes were entered into a container large enough to contain six men, who would crush the grapes with their feet. The liquid would then pour into a smaller trough before being decanted into large, open pottery jars where it fermented. When the fermentation was complete the liquid was transferred to another jar. Often the wine would be siphoned to stop the dregs being mixed with the wine before it was poured.

A timeline for grape cultivation

9000 BC Grape residue found in China
6000 BC Mesopotamia
3000 BC Egypt and Phoenicia
2000 BC Greece
1000 BC Italy, Sicily and North Africa
500 BC Russia, Spain, Portugal and France

Doing as the Romans do

Researchers at the University of Catania in Sicily are carrying out experiments to recreate ancient Roman winemaking skills. The project is a collaboration between the university's archaeology department and the Consiglio Nazionale delle Ricerche (National Research Council).

The academics have turned to original texts in Latin, including those by the Roman poet Virgil, who wrote a treatise on farming called *Georgics*, Pliny the Elder and agriculturalist Columella, in search of guidance for what they should do to make Roman-style wine.

Roman viticulture and winery practice was very sophisticated and advanced. Columella describes 50 varieties of grapevine, although their modern equivalents are not all known. And like modern day vinicultarists the Romans were able to choose varieties to suit climate and soil.

However, not knowing the grape varieties used, the research team decided to plant eight local grape varieties, including Nerello Mascalese, Visparola, Racinedda and Muscatedda.

So in 2013, within sight of Mount Etna in Sicily, a small vineyard was planted from which the researchers hope to harvest 100 kilos of grapes to make 70 litres of wine.

And to make the experiment as realistic as possible, no modern agricultural chemicals are being used, the vines were planted using replicas of Roman tools and were tied to canes as the Romans did.

▼ **Clay amphorae, once used for making and storing wine, can stil be found in many modern vineyards.** (Cath Harries)

The grapes will be macerated gently using bare feet, and the must will be pressed out using screw presses or stone weight presses. The wine will then be fermented by placing it into large terracotta pots which are lined with beeswax to make them waterproof.

The pots, which are large enough to hold a man, are then buried up to the neck and left in the open to ferment, before being sealed shut with clay or resin.

'We will not use fermenting agents, but rely on the fermentation of the grapes themselves, which will make it as hit and miss as it was then – you can call this experimental archaeology,' said researcher Mario Indelicato, who is managing the programme.

'We have found that Roman techniques were more or less in use in Sicily up until a few decades ago, showing how advanced the Romans were. I discovered a two-pointed hoe at my family house on Mount Etna recently that was identical to one we found during a Roman excavation.'

According to the chroniclers of the time, both red and white wines were fermented in contact with the grape skins. They even reduced the wine through evaporation, a technique which stops fermentation, retains sweetness and helps preservation. Four methods were used: sapa, defrutum, caroenum and passum, and clearly the winemakers believed in biodynamics as some of the processes were described as being done during a full moon.

For sapa the wine was reduced by one third; defrutum means reduced by half and aged for a year; caroenum is a reduction to two thirds and passum was a dessert wine of Phoenician origin made from raisins. The reductions were used to sweeten, sour and preserve wine and other foods and drinks. Another technique involved putting a quality red wine in a barrel over a fire which gave the wine a smoky tone.

Once fermented, though the Romans might not know what yeast was, they understood that fermented wine should be removed from the debris at the bottom of a fermenting vessel to stop spoilage or cloudy wines. They also used various filters and finings, including charcoal, albumen, and isinglass, to try to clear wine. And Pliny advised that a duff wine could be refermented blended with fresh must.

However, while evidence shows that the Romans clearly enjoyed drinking wine, an edict was issued in the first century AD prohibiting the planting of new vineyards because farmers had stopped growing wheat.

History of the amphorae

The world has had alcohol ever since the first yeast cells hungrily chomped on to sugars in fruit as a part of their lifecycle. And no doubt early humans, and other animals too, would have eaten rotting fruit and consumed alcohol for the first time.

It is not too big a step to imagine that some people would try to collect the juice in fruit for later consumption. However, if fermentation had started the chances are the liquid would, to us, taste pretty horrible. A fermenting liquid goes sour very quickly when it comes in contact with the air.

The crucial step to making drinkable wine was realising that if a fermented liquid was kept out of contact with the air it remained palatable for much longer.

Animal skins or bladders were probably the first containers for holding wine. It is unclear how effective they were as they would degrade over time but from Homer's *Odyssey* to Shakespeare's plays there are plenty of written references to their uses. But it was the development of the clay pot which was one of the most important developments in the evolution of wine from vinegar to the palatable drink we know today.

The Egyptians and ancient Greeks, as did the Romans, kept their wine, milk, olive oil and grain in large clay vessels called amphorae, which were used to transport goods all over the Greek empire. Amphorae are shaped like long, tapered vases, with a pair of handles at the top. The crucial point is that the pots had a narrow top, which would restrict the amount of air which could come into contact with the liquid inside.

Throughout the Mediterranean and Mesopotamia these clay vessels, which came in many different sizes, were used; they were easy to transport. Besides reducing the surface area of the wine which was exposed to air, the shape enabled sediment to be collected at the bottom, the handles made them easy to carry and they could be buried when cooler long-term storage was needed.

The patron saint of winemaking

Wine is not only said to be the drink of the gods, it has some saintly links too. There have long been close links between the church and winemaking. Indeed, winemakers have their own saint, Vincent Tournante. The venerable saint is still celebrated today – primarily in Burgundy, France, on 22 January, when the region abounds with many religious processions and much merriment.

(Catholic Online)

Across Burgundy there are many societies which honour the different cru wines and terroirs of the region. These brotherhoods of Burgundy come together in long processional parades, which after mass end with a party.

Indeed it is thought that there are now more than 80 St Vincent brotherhoods – mutual aid fraternities set up to help winegrowers obtain assistance from neighbouring vignerons in times of need. The fraternities were first set up in the Middle Ages, with each having a wooden staff to represent the saint which would be carried solemnly throughout the procession.

Over the years celebration and religion have become closely entwined and the day is renowned for the groups of celebrants wearing heavy red robes walking solemnly and sometimes not so solemnly through town and village centres.

It is a big day for the Saint Vincent cooperative, for on this day a statue of Saint Vincent is transferred from the family who presided over the cooperative for 12 months and handed over to the next winegrower family for the year ahead. Pigs will be slaughtered and roasted, some people might attend mass and no doubt much wine will be drunk.

Some say the saint's day traditionally marks the start of pruning of the vines. However, pruning will have begun several weeks before and will continue for some time to come. According to one legend, while wandering the countryside with his donkey, Vincent stopped to talk to some vineyard workers. The donkey ate most of the shoots off the vines, reducing them to stumps. Come harvest time the vines which the donkey had munched its way through had an abundant crop – the best in the vineyard. And thus the need to cut back vine shoots, which can grow many metres long, was discovered.

Another tale is that the saint's name is a corruption of the French words Vin-Sang, which translates into wine-blood. When vines are pruned, they often bleed sap – 'blood' – from the cuts.

The saint's day is celebrated in Croatia too. The vineyards are blessed, bonfires are lit and of course much wine is drunk.

But is there any evidence that Vincent drank wine or wandered Burgundian vineyards in the company of his faithful donkey?

Vincent was born at Huesca, near Saragossa, Spain, sometime during the latter part of the 3rd century. He spent most of his life in Saragossa, became a priest and was appointed by the local bishop, who had a speech impediment, to preach on his behalf across the diocese. However, Vincent's sermons were not liked by some, in particular the governor of the region. He was thrown into jail and asked to renounce his faith. He refused to do so and was tortured on a red hot grid iron, hung on some large sharp hooks and was then starved to death. Quite a death.

According to legend a flock of ravens guarded his body, stopping it being devoured by vultures. Finally, friends retrieved the remains and on its burial the grave too was guarded by a flock of ravens. Eventually, Vincent's body was dug up round 1173 and the bones were distributed across Europe as holy relics.

And Vincent's link with wine? Well, tenuous to say the least.

Saint Urban is also recognised as someone with saintly connections to wine. A bishop of Langres in France during the 4th century, he too was persecuted and hid in a vineyard. Here, he converted workers and then devoted the rest of his life to travelling in France and preaching in vineyards. In France his day is celebrated on 23 January, the day after Vincent's. And if one saint's day is not enough, some celebrate him on 2 April too.

And for those who perhaps had a little too much wine, some might want to say a prayer to the Saints Bibiana and Monica. Bibiana is the patron saint of hangovers – but no one really seems to know why. Like many saints her end in the 4th century was somewhat horrific. According to legend she was tied to a pillar by one of Rome's governors, and was beaten to death after refusing to be converted or be seduced. She died a virgin and a martyr.

Monica was the mother of the drunken St Augustine. She spent many years praying for her feckless but saintly son, a devotion which has seen her named the patron saint of alcoholics.

A short history of English wine

English wines? English grown grapes? Perhaps the questions would have seemed absurd to someone living in England before the Romans came. But today the English (and Welsh) wine industry is a bubbling sensation.

There are now more than 470 vineyards and 135 wineries, and they are making almost 40 million bottles of wine a year.

Currently there are around 1,600 hectares (about 4,000 acres) of grapes being grown, an increase of 140% in the last ten years. England's most northerly vineyard is near York, Yorkshire Heart Vineyard, and the largest single vineyard is Denbies, near Dorking in Surrey, where 106 hectares of grapes are being grown.

We don't know if grapes were grown in England before the first century AD. If they were, the evidence of it has yet to be found. However, wine amphorae have been found in various places across southern England, which does seem to indicate wine could have been drunk. It might seem surprising to us, but there were strong and regular trade links between Britain and the winemaking areas which are now France and Italy.

It was probably members of Belgic tribes who lived in this area before the Romans invaded. Celts it seems preferred to drink mead, ale or other concoctions made with foraged herbs and fruits.

It seems that included in the cargo the invading Romans brought to this country around 43 AD were grapevines. Wherever the Romans went, wine followed. At many sites around the country wine amphorae and drinking cups have been found, and occasionally grape pips and stems of bunches of grapes.

Researchers have identified the remains of seven Romano-British vineyards – four in Northamptonshire, one in Cambridgeshire, one in Lincolnshire and one in Buckinghamshire. One of Roman Britain's biggest vineyards seems to have been in the Nene Valley, in what is now Northamptonshire. Near the village of Wollaston, archaeologists have found about 12 hectares where grapes were grown in a similar style to that found at the same time in the Mediterranean. According to the grape historians more than 4,000 vines were on the site, able to produce 10,000 litres a year, during the 2nd–3rd centuries AD.

However, by the time the Romans began to beat their retreat at the end of the 4th century, knowledge about grape-growing and wine was moving from the Romans to Christian religious orders. It seems that the Jutes, Angles and Saxons were more interested in marauding than growing and fermenting grapes, and probably the Christian communities fled to parts of the British Isles which were far from suitable for growing vines and ripening grapes. But after about 300 years, it seems that as Christianity spread across the country by the 6th century, vine-growing was happening in the south of England again.

And then came the Vikings – which seems to have put a stop to winemaking for another 300 years. However, once King Alfred had stopped burning cakes, he defeated the Vikings and by the 10th century vineyards were being planted again – normally attached to monasteries.

1066 and all that brought viniculture back, because with William the Conqueror came abbots and monks who knew how to grow vines and make wine, and people who wanted to drink it – soldiers, courtiers and civil servants.

The Domesday Book, which was published in 1085, records grapes being grown in 42 different locations. And grape-growing skills had moved out of the monasteries into the estates of the aristocracy, primarily in Gloucestershire, Herefordshire, Somerset and Worcestershire.

For 300 years or so English viticulture prospered. But then it started to decline, due to developments in agriculture, the Black Death and climate change. The dissolution of the monasteries in 1536 probably didn't help, but a new era of farmers preferred other, more profitable crops.

▼ **Winemaking in England is now widespread, sophisticated and has won many plaudits.** (Camel Valley Wines)

Trade between England and France was good – as was seemingly the willingness to do battle with each other. Wine came over in large wooden barrels from France. Henry II (1154–89) had a particular penchant for wines from Bordeaux.

So rather than growing grapes and making wine, business people on these islands turned to what they became world class at – trade. From the 1300s wine was imported, cellared, bottled and resold. London, Bristol and Leith all became renowned as ports into which wine was imported. And classic wine styles including sherry, port, claret, hock and Mosel were all developed during this era.

Though the imports were flooding in, there was some grapegrowing during the 17th century. Lord Salisbury's estate in Hertfordshire made wine of some acclaim. In 1666, John Rose, gardener to Charles II at his Royal Garden in St James's, wrote a detailed paper on the cultivation of vines called *The English Vineyard Vindicated*. Another famed vineyard was Painshill Place, Cobham, Surrey, and vines are still grown here today. But changing consumer tastes – and climate cooling – all saw a decline in English grape-growing.

According to the English Wine Producers the last great experiment into commercial viticulture – that is before the start of the modern revival – was that of Lord Bute at Castel Coch. In 1873, the third Marquess of Bute sent his head gardener Andrew Pettigrew on a boat to France to see how vines should be grown. Following his visit, vines were ordered and in 1875 1.2 hectares were planted at the castle. Over the next 35 years, the original site was expanded and a further two sites were planted.

The Marquess died in 1900. The project kept going, but like many things WW1 saw its demise and by the 1920s the vines were ploughed up. Sadly, farmers could no longer find the workforce to look after not just vines but many other crops.

Then come some dark days. For 30 years or so it seems that grapes were not grown to make wine in England. Two men are credited with the renaissance of the English wine industry: Barrington Brock and Edward Hymans, who both planted small vineyards in the 1950s. Their work inspired Sir Guy Salisbury-Jones who planted a vineyard at Hambledon, north of Portsmouth, in Hampshire.

During the summer of 1951 Sir Guy was looking out of the dining room window of Mill Down House with his stepson

◀ **The third Marquess of Bute revived winemaking in Britain in the 19th century.** (Wikipedia)

John, thinking about what to do with the field directly below them.

As Sir Guy was a keen wine lover and Francophile, having spent time as a diplomat in Paris, John suggested he might consider planting a vineyard. The grape pip had been sown and Sir Guy began researching the feasibility of planting vines on the south-facing chalky slopes.

After careful deliberation, and with the help and advice from friends at the renowned Champagne house Pol Roger, he planted a number of different grape varieties in 1952 and in 1955 the first wine was released. It was the first English wine to be made and sold commercially since the First World War.

Now English and Welsh wine has gone from strength to strength. And it clearly came of age when in 2015, the Queen named the new P&O Cruises vessel *Britannia* at Ocean Terminal, Southampton, on Tuesday, 10 March 2015 by smashing a nebuchadnezzar (the equivalent of 20 bottles) of Wiston Estate Brut NV, which was commissioned for the naming ceremony, on to the ship's hull.

And the rest, as they say, is history. In particular, it is England's bubblies which have been a sparkling success, with many of the judges saying they are better than their French competitors.

▼ **A nebuchadnezzar of English bubbly, not French, helped launch the cruise ship Britannia.** (P&O Cruises)

English King Henry VIII had a penchant for French wine.
(Historic Royal Palaces/Richard Lea-Hair)

Grape history –
in the court of the Tudor King

The Tudor elite drank wine, and like the rest of the population, young and old, they drank beer too or what they then called ale.

Yes, many in the 17th century were bon viveurs. Recently at Hampton Court in West London a wine fountain was installed in the main courtyard so that people could have wine on tap. Historians say it is similar to a water fountain, the base of which was discovered in the palace in 2008 during archaeological works undertaken before the courtyard was restored. According to the historians such temporary fountains, made for feasts and revels on high days and holidays, didn't just dispense fresh water, but wine too. The octagonal structure is similar in ground plan to the wine fountain in the Field of the Cloth of Gold painting, although smaller.

At Anne Boleyn's four-day coronation extravaganza in 1533, wine fountains were set up in London's Gracechurch Street, Cheapside and Fleet Street, and fountains also featured at Queen Elizabeth I's coronation. In Oxford and Cambridge, when the dons at the colleges were entertaining royalty, fountains were set up too.

The Tudor-style wine replica fountain at Hampton Court was 4.3 metres high and can hold up to 320 litres of wine. The wine came from the same area where good King Henry got most of his wine, Gascony. And the king had barrels of it: according to the records, 15,000 gallons were kept at Hampton Court at any one time.

Oxford Archaeology project manager Ben Ford said: 'Oxford Archaeology excavated Base Court at Hampton Court Palace and found the brick foundations to an octagonal fountain, constructed by Cardinal Wolsey c1520.

▲ **Interior of Henry VIII's Wine Cellar.** (Nicola Twilley)

'A lead water pipe, much like other water pipes found at the palace, indicated this was a water fountain with no evidence of it having been used for wine.'

Henry VIII's palace possessed a sophisticated water system supplied by means of buried lead pipes from springs three miles away at Coombe Hill. This served a number of fountains, including an elaborate fountain built by Henry in Clock Court and a smaller fountain – or conduit – in Base Court.

However, Ford went on to explain, 'The Historic Royal Palaces who look after Hampton Court wanted to create a visitor attraction, so constructed a replica of the wine fountain represented in the painting of a meeting between Henry VIII and the French king at the Field of the Cloth of Gold in 1520 – this meeting was organised by Wolsey.

'This was a temporary affair designed for diplomacy and to show off. Henry had a false brick palace built from flatpacked timber elements and real glass. Tents had gold thread woven into their fabric. The wine fountain should be viewed in this context.

'We did not study historic references to wine fountains, as ours was a water fountain, but apparently there was one at the coronation of Anne Boleyn.'

And while the temporary structure was open, it ran with red and chilled white wine.

'We've used original Tudor images of wine fountains and Hampton Court's wealth of surviving architectural detail to recreate something truly unique,' said the Historic Royal Palaces historian in charge of the project, Dr Kent Rawlinson, curator of Historic Buildings at Hampton Court.

'Hampton Court was a "pleasure palace" for Henry VIII, where

guests were entertained with spectacular revels and festivities, and wine and beer were drunk in enormous quantities, as evidenced by the great cellars that still survive here.'

HENRY VIII'S WHITEHALL WINE CELLAR

In the centre of London, under the Ministry of Defence building in Whitehall, can be found another of Henry VIII's wine cellars, one of the few remaining parts of Whitehall Palace – the main London residence of England's kings and queens for more than 150 years.

Once, Whitehall was the biggest and grandest palace in Europe, dwarfing both the Vatican and Versailles and covering more than nine hectares between the River Thames and Green Park. It must have been quite a place as by 1650, the palace was the largest complex of non-church buildings in England, with over 1,500 rooms.

Whitehall became a royal palace after Henry VIII confiscated it from Cardinal Wolsey, when he failed to annul the king's wedding to Catherine of Aragon. At the same time Henry also took over Hampton Court. And clearly the king and his court must have drunk plenty of wine as the cellar is big at about 20 metres by nine metres.

The palace could have still been with us today, but it was gutted in 1698 and left as a ruin, with very little remaining – though the Tudor wine cellar with its brick-vaulted roof did survive. Somehow it has survived to the present day – and this even included being moved in 1949, when it was encased

▲ The 'Great Vine', planted at Hampton Court Palace in 1768 by Lancelot 'Capability' Brown. (Historic Royal Palaces/newsteam.co.uk)

▶ Jill Cox, vinekeeper, cuts grapes from the 'Great Vine'.
(Historic Royal Palaces/newsteam.co.uk)

in steel and concrete, moved three metres to the west and sunk a further six metres as part of a massive rebuilding of the site. The bricks were so soft that any attempt to dismantle the room to move it and rebuild it would have failed. Sadly, the cellar is not often open to the public though it is sometimes used by the Ministry of Defence.

WORLD'S OLDEST VINE

Hampton Court has an important role to play in the vine's grape history. It is home to the world's oldest and some say biggest vine, which was planted in 1769. Most commercial vines are unlikely to be older than 30 years old.

It was planted by one of the world's first celebrity gardeners, Capability Brown, from a cutting taken from a Black Hamburg vine at Valentines Mansion in Essex. By 1887 it measured 1.2 metres around the base. It is now four metres around the base and the longest rod is 36.5 metres. The vine is grown on the extension method where one plant fills a glasshouse. In Victorian times gardeners thought that a larger crop was produced this way.

Old the vine may be, but it still produces more than 270kg a year and in autumn 2001 had its largest crop of 383kg. It has outgrown its greenhouse on several occasions and had to have a new one built around it – the last time being in 1969.

How bug wars blighted wine

This is a story of how human intervention all but destroyed Europe's wine industry and human ingenuity saved it.

The problem was a creepy crawly bug imported from North America, sometime during the 19th century, which all but destroyed Europe's vineyards – indeed, France's wine industry was withering on the grapevine.

In the middle to late 1800s travel across the Atlantic was easy. The new, state of the art, steam powered iron hulls could power across the Atlantic in just eight days carrying 1,500 passengers and 5,000 tonnes of cargo. And it wasn't just people and manufactured goods which passed from coast to coast. So did plants, animals and bugs.

In the 1870s, phylloxera, a devastating aphid-like yellow bug, was introduced on vines imported from America to Europe. It attacked the roots and all but wiped out most of the continent's vines, including some of the greatest vineyards in France.

France became the unwanted home for the deadly insect known as Phylloxera Vastatrix. It's a tiny, voracious beetle which feeds on the roots of vines, causing fungal infection, root deformation and eventually their death.

Viniculture had taken root in California around the 1800s, and it thrived, with England in particular being a huge importer of concentrated must, to which water was added to make wine.

But phylloxera wasn't the first unwanted grape disease to cross the Atlantic. Around the 1830s a powdery mildew, called oidium, made the eastward crossing to Europe. Evidence of it was recorded by an English gardener known as Edward Tucker who noticed how a white, dusty fungus spread through his grapes and destroyed them.

By the 1850s the fungus had crossed the Channel and was spreading through French vineyards, where it was particularly partial to Sauvignon and Chardonnay grapes. Within a few short years the fatal fungus had spread to most vineyards in Europe. During this time, French wine production fell from 11 million to 3 million hectolitres. Across Europe the fate of the wine industry hung in the balance.

Thankfully, by the 1850s plant scientists discovered that by spraying vines with a sulphur compound the downy mildew could be, if not eradicated, held in check. However, by this time the loss of their crops had persuaded many winegrowers to rip up their vines in order to plant supposedly oidium-resistant Vitis vinifera varieties, or hybrid varieties, which were imported from America.

Little did they know that the supposed healthy vine stock harboured an even more deadly enemy, phylloxera. The beetle, which became known as the dreaded dry-leaf devastator, may have arrived on vines imported by English plant hunters at some time in the 1850s; other say a Monsieur Borty imported American vine cuttings, and planted them in his Rhône vineyards in 1862. The bug thrived in the soil in which most of Europe's vines were planted, however in North America it co-existed more benignly with the vines it liked to live on.

Whatever the truth is, the bugs went on to gorge their way through Europe's vineyards, starting in Rhône, and the glory years of wine production were over.

Vineyards across France were devastated and winemakers were struggling financially as vines languished and died.

▼ **A small bug imported from the US devastated Europe's vineyards.** (Phylloxera Institute Francais)

▼ **Oidium was the first grape disease to cross the Atlantic to devastate vines in Europe.** (Phylloxera Institute Francais)

Hundreds of people were put out of work and land cultivated with vines for generations lay unused.

All manner of chemical coshes were invoked to curb the advance of the bug. And if pesticides didn't work, toads, chickens and other animals were employed to see if they would eat the bugs.

None of it worked – clearly root and branch reform was needed. But then some canny scientist heard on the grapevine that the solution might lie back across the Atlantic where the bug was endemic. Here vines were not being devastated by the underground beasty.

Europe's great wineries were only saved when botanists realised that they could graft Europe's fine, wine-bearing vines on to American root stock which are immune to phylloxera.

It worked – so, a problem created by people was also solved by people. However, not everyone was happy and to this day some still say the solution destroyed the character of Europe's fine wine.

DOGS TO SNIFF OUT VINE KILLER

Few parts of the world managed to stay free of phylloxera. It cannot survive in very sandy soils, so the great plains of Hungary and Colares in Portugal were immune from attack. Chile, protected by the Andes and Pacific Ocean, has also remained free of the bug.

However, a whining dog could help ensure some of the world's grapevines grow disease free. University of Melbourne viticulture and animal science researcher Sonja Needs has combined her two passions, dogs and wine, to train sniffer dogs to detect vineyard diseases, especially phylloxera.

South Australia is currently phylloxera free, and would like to keep it that way, as is a small area of the Yarra Valley. Needs says it is possible to train any breed to be a sniffer dog and it was a case of taking a dog already trained in other services, like drug detection, and 'flicking their switch' to instead detect vine pests such as phylloxera.

'Once they are trained in detection, it's a very simple thing to give them another scent and they just work,' Needs said. 'And they love it, it's a fun activity for them and we love doing it because it's fun for us too.'

Needs said she was particularly interested in at what stage of the lifecycle the dogs could detect phylloxera. When they

sniff out the bugs the dogs start to energetically wag their tails, bark and whine.

'Because phylloxera is on the roots inside the soil, I want to see at what depth the dogs can pick them up – maybe a metre below the surface,' she said. 'And if they can it's going to be an amazingly powerful detection tool.'

If the scientist is right then dogs could be used to patrol the edges of phylloxera-free zones and sniff viticulture equipment before it is moved, making sure that the pest is not spread.

▼ **Trained dogs could soon be used to sniff out vines infected with phylloxera.** (Cath Harries)

Seaing is believing – can wine be stored under the ocean waves?

Some winemakers have been experimenting with storing wine underneath the sea to see how it affects ageing. Some of the world's finest wines are stored in cool, dark caves for many years to bring out the best in them.

But the winemakers from the Mira winery wanted to try something different – well they do come from California. So in 2013 they decided to sink a bottle or two of their 2009 Cabernet Sauvignon into Charleston Harbor to see what effect underwater ageing would have.

They aren't the first to do it. Some years back, in July 2010, 140 bottles of wine were found unopened in a two-centuries-old shipwreck, the *Åland*, which sank in the Baltic Sea.

Some of it was champagne which came from the Veuve Clicquot estate and the now long gone Juglar house. The bottles were originally destined for quaffing at the Russian Imperial Court. Instead the consignment, which included 47 bottles of Veuve Clicquot from 1839 and 1841, ended up in Davy Jones' locker.

On tasting some were described by experts as being in exquisite condition. And indeed one of the bottles of champagne was sold at auction to a Singaporean collector for more than £26,000.

▶ **A collector of wine bought a bottle of the under-sea champagne for £26,000.** (Visit *Åland*)

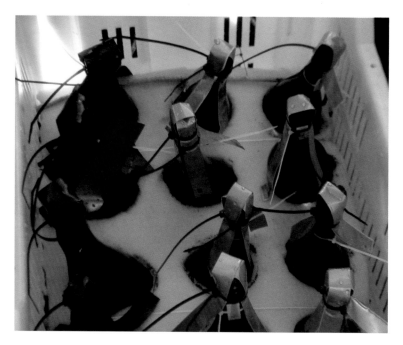

▲ Veuve Clicquot deliberately sank bottles of its rosé in an underwater cellar.
(Visit *Åland*)

▼ After a life under the ocean waves, the wine proved to be very drinkable.
(Mira Winery)

Next, in 2011, Veuve Clicquot decided to deliberately submerge a selection of its vintage Yellow Label and Vintage Rosé 2004 in an underwater cellar in the sea. The bubbly was submerged 40 metres down close to the wreck of the *Åland*, as part of a 50-year ageing experiment.

Meanwhile, bottles from the same vintages are being kept in the champagne house's chalk cellar – at 2° to 4°C, the same temperature as the Baltic. And the champagne-makers say they will be making regular comparisons between the two stores – so they can monitor any changes and differences between the cellar and the sea.

Then, the Drappier champagne house decided to immerse 600 bottles of its Brut and 60 bottles of Grand Sendrée 2005 into Saint-Malo bay off France. Here it was kept, 15 metres down, at temperatures of 7° to 9°C.

So not to be outdone, Mira's winemakers wanted to have a go at undersea maturation in a project known as Aquaoir. Mira Winery President Jim Dyke Jr wanted to see how wine would be affected if aged in the ocean, and was experimenting with the major elements that can

affect maturation – temperature, humidity, pressure, motion, light – or lack thereof – and oxygen. He says the experiment follows generations of European wineries that have explored the ocean's impact on wine.

After three months the bottles were retrieved and one tasted. 'The land wine is tighter versus Aquaoir-aged wine, which is more complex and broad, more open and relaxed. The result is proof certain that we have more to learn,' said Dyke.

'There is no doubt that the ocean holds a potential gift to wine. The success of Phase I makes us more committed than ever to going back down in the fall with twice the cages for twice the time,' he said.

In November 2014, in Phase III of the project, a further seven cases of wine were sunk below the waves, including a bottle or two of Chardonnay. However, the winery's saline experimentation might have been bought to an end by the US Treasury Department's Alcohol and Tobacco Tax and Trade Bureau. It has warned that potential contact with seawater would render the wines adulterated and thus illegal to sell. The bureau, which oversees alcohol labelling, can ban wineries selling or shipping their products if they are judged to have been contaminated in some way.

According to the bureau all manner of nasties including gasoline, oil, heavy metals, plastics, drug residues, pesticides, as well as various types of filth, including waste materials from biological sources, sludge, decaying organic matter, runoff from farms, effluents from sewage treatment plants, and bilge waters from vessels could enter the bottles via the cork.

Dyke has put a brave face on the latest development and said he was disappointed with the news. Perhaps the government officials should have gone to one of the tastings of Dyke's previous submersions, when all those tasted were given the all clear. Indeed one of the expert tasters whimsically said 'something magical has happened with Aquaoir'.

Perhaps the Fed officials were more head than heart, and had come to their view on the basis of press stories of a tasting of a 150-year-old wine or spirit which was found in a wreck in Charleston Harbor. It was one of five bottles recovered by divers from the *Mary-Celestia*, an iron-hulled paddle steamship that sank under mysterious circumstances during the US Civil War.

A panel of sommeliers really had the sinking feeling when they came to taste it. When the bottle was uncorked they weren't impressed and said the cloudy yellow-grey liquid smelled and tasted like a mixture of crab water, gasoline, salt water and vinegar, with hints of citrus and alcohol.

Clearly, we will need to see results before we know the long-term effects of wine bottles spending part of their life under the ocean waves.

The scientific verdict

Scientific analysis of the contents of three of the bottles found in the Baltic produced some surprising results. Professor Philippe Jeandet from the University of Reims in Champagne-Ardenne took the bottles of Veuve Clicquot and carried out a chemical analysis of the liquid, discovering very high levels of sugar and traces of arsenic.

Many of the wine's chemical features were preserved thanks to the 'close to perfect' ageing conditions of the cold and dark seabed. Such conditions had preserved the Champagne 'allowing the scientists to shed light on 19th-century winemaking'.

The professor said: 'Composition of 170-year-old Champagne samples found in a shipwreck in the Baltic Sea constitutes a remarkable and unprecedented example of long-term combinatorial chemistry, which can occur in such sealed 750ml micro laboratories.'

The main difference was the sugar content, which was about 150g per litre (more than most Sauternes), compared to today's Champagnes which are generally between 6 to 10g per litre. At the time Russians liked their wine to be sweet and would often add sugar to a glass when drinking it.

The scientists believe that the traces of arsenic probably came from arsenic slats used to control bugs in vineyards.

CHAPTER 2
THE WINE STORY

Happy vines make bad wines

First, find some growing vines and when ripe harvest the grapes. Then squash the berries, collect the juice and wait.

The Vitus genus has many family members, but it is primarily *Vitis vinifera* that winemakers seek. The vinifera species evolved thousands of years ago from wild vines growing in Asia. In the wild, the plants grow long, tall and clambering in an effort to haul themselves above the towering tree canopy.

At the end of the vine's spindly tendrils, pushing their way towards the clouds, buds, flowers and then grapes form. The grapes are a welcome source of food for birds, bugs and tree climbing animals, which picked them straight from the vine or foraged them after they had fallen to the forest floor. And in the fullness of time the pips would be excreted and life's circle of germination, growth and fruit would begin again.

▲ **In the wild, vines would grow long and tall, searching for the sky.** (Wine Argentina)

◀ **Vines pruned in single Royat cordon.** (Burgundy Tourism)

A modern grape-grower doesn't rely on accidents of nature or serendipity to grow new vines, for today most new vines are clones or crossings of an existing species, which is then grafted on to a phylloxera-free American rootstock.

And the winemaker won't let the vine waste energy on growing tall as they once did in the wild – far better the plants' efforts are put into growing rich, luscious fruits. So most commercial vines are harshly pruned back to encourage fruit growth.

WHERE ARE VINES GROWN?

Vines can be grown in most parts of the world. But commercial growing is roughly concentrated into two broad bands in the north and south of the planet roughly between 30 and 50 degrees of latitude. It is in these areas that the right amounts of heat and cold, sunshine and rainfall can be found. Elsewhere the vines might grow but the conditions are not right for the fruits to develop enough of the fermentable sugars the winemaker needs.

▼ **Vines at Assmannshausen in winter.** (GNTB/Rüdesheim Tourist AG)

Grape-growers spend a lot of time looking at weather forecasts – grapes don't grow when the temperature is below 10°C. In the northern hemisphere vines are mostly dormant from November to March.

The type of vine originally grown in an area was often swayed by the climate – is the spring early or late? When will the frosts arrive in winter? Some varieties, like Pinot Noir, bud early and could be susceptible to late frost. Riesling often ripens later, so a cold, wet autumn could be a disaster for the winemaker.

The closeness of water can also make a difference. A river, lake or sea can make the climate less extreme in hotter parts of the world.

VINE-GROWING

In most of Europe the grape variety planted is governed by custom, trial and error and law. Growers in the New World are not constrained by either law or tradition and will grow the variety which they think is appropriate to the wine they want to make.

To prosper grapes need sunshine, more than 1,500 hours

◄ The best grapes grow in ground which looks unpromising. (Mills Reef Winery Ltd)

of it, and usually some pretty warm weather to make the grapes grow sugary sweet.

The art of the grower is to produce a variety which has the level of sugar, acid and tannin they need for the wine they are making.

SOIL CONDITIONS

The best grapes are probably grown in ground which looks most unpromising. Few growers are looking for humus rich soil; instead they starve the vines and force them to grow in hard, flinty granite soils, or other uncompromising environments which are pretty much unsuitable for anything else. The grower wants the vine to put most of its energy into the developing fruit. Commercial vines are not expected to reach up through a tree canopy and touch the sky.

Growers will tell you that limestone and chalk are best for Chardonnay, elegant crisp Rieslings prefer slate and Cabernet likes well drained gravel.

The roots force their way deep into the rock in search of nutrients and water. As the grapes ripen, acidity decreases and the sugars increase. And in the struggle for life – energy goes into the production of rich, sugar-full grapes.

LIGHT AND HEAT ARE IMPORTANT

In cooler areas vines will be planted on slopes which catch the warmth of the midday sun. Growers in Burgundy like south-eastwards facing slopes, so that their vines warm under the morning sun. In Germany where cold morning mists embrace the hillsides, growers seek out south-westward locations so they benefit from the heat of the afternoon sun.

In the hottest climates vines will be spaced apart so the excesses of heat dissipate quickly and easily. In cooler places the vines stand close together, like penguins in an Antarctic storm. This conserves heat. The vines will be cut low and trained so the prevailing wind finds it hard to blow the essential heat away.

THE EUROPEAN UNION

The European Union (EU) has divided Europe into six different winemaking regions which are loosely based on the climate of the region, with Zone A the coolest and Zone C III b the warmest.

As a rough guide, white wines are more likely to be grown in the cooler areas, and different grape varieties prosper in different regions.

In the EU the winegrowing region also determines whether certain winemaking practices, which might be banned or frowned upon in other regions, can happen. One such is chaptalisation: the process of adding sugar to unfermented grape must in order to increase the alcohol content after fermentation.

England and parts of Germany in Zone A are the coolest, and chaptalisation can happen and the wines may be de-acidified. This could increase the alcoholic strength of wine by up to 4.5% ABV.

The south of Spain, Italy and Portugal are the warmest in Zone C III b – chaptalisation and de-acidification are illegal, but tartaric acid may be added to increase the acidity of a wine.

OTHER SYSTEMS

The University of California, Davis, has developed a heat summation guide to show which grape varietals would grow in California, and the system is now used in other parts of the world.

It is a system which relies on something called the degree-day. The average daily temperature is monitored between 1 April and 31 October. The degree-day value in Fahrenheit is derived by subtracting 50 from the day's average. (50°F is the minimum temperature for grape-growing.) The values for each day in the period are added together to determine the region's classification.

The UC Davis scale is divided into five levels. Region I is the coolest and Region V is the warmest.

- **Region I:** Below 2,500 degree days – Chardonnay, Pinot Noir, Gewürztraminer, Riesling
- **Region II:** 2,500–3,000 degree days – Cabernet Sauvignon, Merlot, Sauvignon Blanc
- **Region III:** 3,000–3,500 degree days – Zinfandel, Barbera, Gamay
- **Region IV:** 3,500–4,000 degree days – Malvasia, some varieties of table grapes such as sultanas
- **Region V:** Over 4,000 degree days – Table grapes.

▼ **Europe's grape growing regions determine certain winemaking practices.** (EuroGraphics)

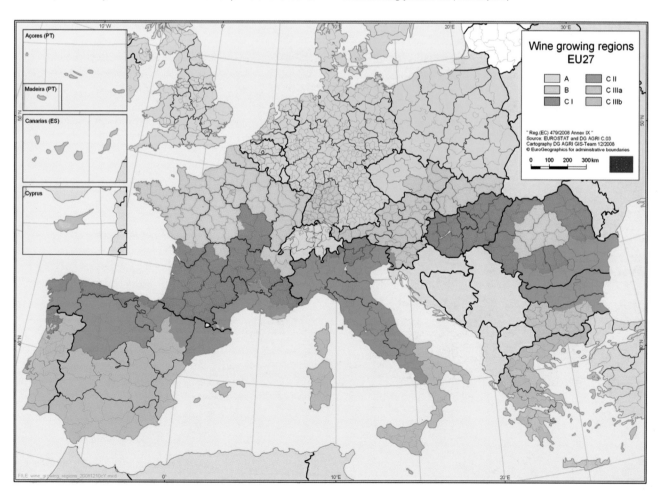

Major grape varieties

There are thousands of varieties of grapes from which wine could be made. Indeed in some vineyards, the growers have no idea of the variety they are growing, and they just give a shrug of their shoulders when asked. However, most wine in the world is probably made from 20 or so of varieties – here are some of them.

WHITE GRAPES

Aligote

One of the grapes which made Burgundy famous. It was first recorded as a variety in the 18th century. Vintners say its output is best in warm dry years. The juice is high in acidity and suitable for wines which will be drunk young. Today, it is also grown in Bulgaria, California and Moldavia. Its juice along with lashings of blackcurrant liqueur is found in Kir.

Chardonnay

The grape variety that has become so well-known it's become a brand in its own right. It will probably grow anywhere, but it likes chalky soils. It is grown worldwide and can be found in Australia, California, Chile, New Zealand and South Africa. It's a vital component of white Burgundies and Champagnes as well as being a staple for supermarkets and wine bars. Many drinkers will walk into a bar and just order a 'Chardonnay' when they cannot think of anything else to say. Winemakers say when over-ripe the grapes give excessive sweetness at the expense of acidity. It gives wine green apple flavours when grown in cooler climates. If aged in wood it brings out buttery flavours.

Chasselas

Could this be a grape with a lineage back to ancient Egypt? Some experts believe it so. A favourite for the fruit bowl, it has fallen out of favour with most winemakers. Under other names (Fendant and Weisser Gutedel) it is often used as a key component of light wines in Switzerland and Germany. It is also used in blended wines from Alsace.

▼ **Machine harvesting in the Chablis region.** (Burgundy Tourism)

Chenin Blanc

One of the winemaker's workhorses, which could probably turn its hand to almost any wine style, be it dry, sweet, still or sparkling. Widely grown in the Loire Valley in France, it also prospers under the hot sun of South Africa. Winemakers like to use it in wines for ageing.

Gewürztraminer

Is it French or German? Some say its origins are Italian. It is primarily grown in Alsace, though it has tendrils in many countries. It is a classic and marvellous mainstay of many of the wines from Alsace. It can be used for late harvest ultra-sweet wines because it ages well. It is also grown in Australia, California and New Zealand. Confusingly, gewürz means spice in German, but its attributes tend to lean more towards tropical fruit. Down under, in Australia, it is often blended with Riesling.

Malvasia

An ancient family of grapes which can be used to produce most forms of wine – white or red, still or sparkling, dry or sweet. It seems to grow well in winegrowing areas which are the hottest and have the poorest soils.

Muscadet – Melon de Bourgogne

Would we have wine from the Loire without this grape? Its must produces dry, crisp and some say characterless wines. Wines made with it are often served chilled and coincidentally the vines thrive in the frosty conditions found in the Loire region. It is also beloved by distillers.

Muscat

More a family than one grape variety, its taxonomy is widely regarded as making a wine that tastes of grapes. Apparently most wines made from grapes don't. Serious wine buffs seek out Muscat Blancs à Petits Grains and Muscat Ottonel grapes. When blended it produces light, aromatic and fruity wines. The late harvest grapes are intensely sweet.

Palomino

Anyone who has ever drunk a sherry has tasted this grape. A favourite in Spain, it doesn't add much to wine as it lacks acidity and fruit. However, it comes into its own when matured in a solera, which unleashes intense, aromatic sherry flavours. For sherry-style winemakers from South Africa, California and Australia, it's a wolf in a sheep's clothing.

Pedro Ximenez

There is something mysterious about this grape. It plays a starring part in the sweet fortified sherries of Jerez, Spain, which sees the grapes dried before fermentation to concentrate the sweetness. Many winemakers say its low acidity makes it a poor grape to use in an everyday wine. It is

widely planted in Argentina. It is also grown in Portugal, where it is known as Perrum and is used in blends.

Pinot Blanc

It's the grape world's equivalent of the Ford Transit van. It does a lot of hard graft and is very versatile. Widely grown in Alsace, it is often thought to be synonymous with Chardonnay. Well it is not, though it can be as ubiquitous. Vin ordinaire, it might be, it produces light, crisp, yeasty-zesty wines with apple blossom, honey and mineral flavours. It grows best on poor chalky, limey soils.

Pinot Gris

An Alsace favourite, where it is called Tokay Pinot Gris, and in Italy, where we know it as Pinot Grigio. It is also grown in Oregon in the US and New Zealand. Italian versions tend to be unassertive and bland, but highly drinkable. The French growths in the best years are said to age well and produce beautiful buttery wines. It ripens early and has a high sugar content.

Prosecco

Fast becoming the world's favourite sparkling wine, the main component of the blend is the Prosecco grape, which is also known as Glera. It is unusual for the name of a grape, the wine it makes and the region it comes from (north of Venice) to be the same. It makes immensely popular non-vintage, drink anytime, anywhere bubbly wines.

Riesling

Most of Germany's greatest wines use Riesling grapes. It is renowned for its harmony of intense acidity and floral-fruity aromas. It can be found in crisp bone dry wines and intensely sweet wines. It is now also widely grown in Australia, New Zealand and South Africa. It is frost tolerant.

Sauvignon Blanc, Fumé Blanc

Widely grown in Bordeaux and the Loire Valley, it is often blended with Semillon to produce crispy dry, aromatic white wines. It has also become a favourite in New World wines, with successful plantings in Chile and New Zealand. It adds acidity to sweet Sauternes. In New Zealand it makes wines with penetrating fruit flavours. It is also grown in Chile and South Africa.

Semillon

Typically found in crisp, bone dry blends from Bordeaux and the Loire Valley. It is widely planted worldwide and is the prime grape for Sauternes. The grape is said to age well and some believe wines made from it are best drunk when at least five years old. It ferments well and makes strong wines which are low in acidity and aroma. It also ages well in oak.

Silvaner/Sylvaner

Once widely planted in Germany and Alsace, its use is now in decline, being replaced by better yielding Pinot Blanc and Riesling. Wines made with it are usually high in acidity and low in fruity aromas.

Trebbiano

Grown in south-east France and Italy on land usually close to the Mediterranean. It is widely used in Italy as a component of white and red blends. A high yield grape, it is favoured by distillers and is found in both Armagnac and Cognac.

Welschriesling

With a good frost tolerance, its young wines have fruity notes of currant or gooseberry. It is a component of some sparkling wines and is widely grown in central Europe and northern Italy. It is popular in Slovakia and the Czech Republic. It is no relation to the Riesling grape.

▼ **One of the most influential factors affecting the flavour of wine is the grape variety, or varieties, used.** (Cath Harries)

BLACK OR RED GRAPES

Barbera

Extensively grown in northern Italy, it is also found in California where it thrives on poor quality chalky soils. Widely used in wines which are best drunk young. It produces wines with a deep ruby colour which are low in tannins and high in acidity. It can age well.

Cabernet Sauvignon

Probably the world's best known red wine grape, it will grow successfully on many types of soil. In Bordeaux it is famed for its contribution to wines from the Médoc and Graves. Wines made from it are often characterised by intense blackcurrant flavours. It ages well and produces wines which are big in tannins. It is widely used in deep, red, full-bodied and aged wines.

Carignan/Cariñena

The grape's Spanish heritage hasn't stopped it being widely grown in France. It is also found in Italy and Mexico. It thrives on poor soils and is commonplace in many everyday, easy-drinking wines. Many growers are now replacing it with grapes which produce more complex wines. It adds acidity and intense colour to blends.

Frankovka

A late ripening grape found in central and eastern Europe. It produces wine with an intense ruby colour. As it ages its high acidity softens, revealing dark red fruit and spicy, leather flavours.

Gamay

Widely grown in Burgundy, it is the go-to grape for many winemakers and predominates in Beaujolais Nouveau. It makes easy-drinking wines, but also contributes to wines with a little age, producing mellow blackcurrant notes and tinges of purple.

Grenache

There are probably more Grenache vines growing in the world than any other. It is a key element of many blends. When blended with Cabernet Sauvignon it produces wines of great complexity and sophistication. It is widely used in Australia.

Malbec

Also known as Côt Noir and Auxerrois, Malbec is grown in parts of south-west France, where it is used along with Merlot and Tannat to produce the characteristic dark red, almost black wines from the Cahors region. It is successfully grown in South America, with Argentinian Malbec being a particularly well-regarded varietal.

▲ **Malbec grapes growing in Argentina.** (Wines of Argentina)

Merlot

If you are in Bordeaux and you see a red grapevine growing, it is probably Merlot. Easy to grow, it survives in most soil conditions but needs aggressive pruning if it is to produce the best grapes. Quick maturing, it produces wines which are low in tannin and with a gentle, soft raspberry fruitiness. It is grown in most of the world's winegrowing regions and produces some vinous stars in California and Chile.

Nebbiolo

The classic red grape of northern Italy. Its name derives from the Italian word for fog, nebbia. Winemakers say it is difficult to grow as it flowers and ripens early. However, it produces grapes which are full of sugar, acidity and tannins. It prospers if aged for ten years or more producing wines with intense floral, liquorice and tobacco flavours.

Pinot Noir

Young wines made with this grape are characterised by soft red fruit flavours and a pale red colour. When aged it turns brick red, with scents of plum jam and leather. Low yielding, it produces famed wines in Burgundy and though it is widely planted worldwide few other growers manage to achieve these sublime heights. However, vintages from California and New Zealand have been acclaimed. To the surprise of many it is used as a blending wine in Champagne.

Sangiovese

A favourite in Italy, it plays a starring role in Chianti. For some years, poor grape husbandry led to it being over-cropped, which produced wines which lacked a fulsome character. However, better management has seen its star rise once more with people relishing the high acidity and rasping levels of tannin.

Syrah/Shiraz

When grown in Australia and South Africa it produces complex, intense wines, layered with flavours of spice and pepper. Rich and plummy, it is a major contributor to some of the world's best red wines such as Châteauneuf du Pape and Gigondas. New World variants tend to be sweeter than those grown in Europe.

Tempranillo

If you are drinking a Rioja it is likely to include this grape. A Spanish favourite, it grows in most of the country other than the very south, where the intensity of the sunshine curbs its progress. It is also found in Portugal and Argentina. The grape brings spicy, leather and tobacco notes to wines. Winemakers say the grape's best characteristics are revealed if the wine is stored in oak for several years.

Zinfandel

A Californian favourite, the sunshine state has made this grape its own. Its popularity has risen with the growth in the drinking of blush wines. It ages well in American oak barrels, which bring pronounced vanilla notes to the wine. It is used for wines of all styles from soft whites to robust ports.

So what's in a grape?

The essential part of the vine is the grape berry, which is made up of skin, pulp, and seeds.

The skin is made up of six to ten layers of thick-walled cells. The skin provides the winemaker with red and yellow colours, tannins, aromatics and potassium and other minerals. Thicker-walled grapes are often best for growing in areas with hard winter frosts.

The pulp is mainly plant cells containing the juice. The juice is mostly water – about 70 to 80% of it in fact. The other stuff contains different sugars, organic acids, and other material including phenolics, nitrogenous compounds, aromatics, minerals and pectic materials. When the grape is gently crushed the juice is released.

And at the centre of the grape are the seeds, which are also rich in tannins, which add character to many red wines.

SWEET SUCCESS

Sucrose, glucose and fructose are the main sugars found in a grape plant. The sucrose is created in the plant by photosynthesis as it grows. The sugar is a source of energy for the plant which helps create the grapes.

For the most part, sugars exist in the vine as sucrose, a molecule of glucose and fructose. However, upon reaching the grape the sucrose splits into glucose and fructose.

In unripe grapes glucose predominates. In overripe grapes fructose dominates. At the fully ripened stage, glucose and fructose are usually present in equal amounts. In overripe grapes the concentration of fructose exceeds that of glucose.

Glucose, fructose and sucrose all differ significantly in sweetness. The order of sweetness is: fructose is sweeter than sucrose, which is sweeter than glucose.

It is important for winemakers to know the levels of the different sugars. For a sweet wine, the winemaker will need less fructose than sucrose to reach the same degree of sweetness. And different grape varieties have different proportions of the sugars – for instance, when ripe, Chardonnay and Pinot Blanc are usually high in fructose, while Chenin Blanc and Zinfandel are high in glucose.

MEASURING RIPENESS

A refractometer is usually used to measure the ripeness and sweetness of a grape. A drop of grape juice is placed between two prisms. The way the light travels and bends (refracts) through the prisms and juice can be used to measure the amount of sugar present.

The reading from the bending light is measured as a value on the Brix scale. Pure water with no sugar has a Brix value of zero, while water with sugars has a higher Brix value. Most wine grapes are harvested at between 21 and 25 Brix. Sweet wines, like Sauternes, will be much higher.

To get a rough idea of alcohol content of the final wine, multiply the stated Brix by 0.55.

FERMENTATION

During fermentation, the yeast converts sugars to alcohol and carbon dioxide. The amount of alcohol produced is related to the amount of sugar initially present in the juice; thus, by controlling the amount of sugar in the juice, the winemaker can control the amount of alcohol in the wine.

▼ **A refractometer is used to measure the levels of ripeness and sweetness of a grape.** (Weiku)

▲ **Vines pruned on the double cordon system.** (Burgundy Tourism)

Vines – a cutting experience

The shape of the commercial grapevine is governed by the way in which it is pruned.

The main pruning of a vine in both the northern and southern hemispheres takes place in the early winter when the plant will be severely cut back. However, it will continue throughout the spring and summer when the vines will be trained, some new shoots will be pinched out and the fruits will be thinned.

The aim of pruning is to keep the vine's growth under control and have most of its energy directed into the bunches of grapes. It is also a way of controlling the leaf growth so that the burgeoning grapes are exposed to sunlight, or if needed, shade in very hot climates. Also, pruning aids the ventilation of the plant, as usually the better the circulation of air the less likely potential for fungus.

Pruning is also used to position the growing grapes nearer to the ground or further away from it. In some vine-growing areas, growers hasten the ripening of their fruits by positioning the bunches close to the ground so that the sunshine reflects off the rocky soil on to the grapes.

In humid areas, grapes will be often grown further away from the ground; this encourages air circulation and reduces the likelihood of the grapes rotting.

THE PRUNING SYSTEMS

The three principal pruning systems are the Guyot system, rod and spur or cordon system, and the bush.

Guyot

The Guyot system of training sees either one or two fruiting arms growing from the main stem – the single or double system.

The main stem will be cut back to two healthy buds above the graft. For a single Guyot, one single shoot is tied to the lowest horizontal wire on the growing frame, either to the left or right. For a double Guyot, one shoot is tied to the left and one to the right along the lowest wire.

Rod and spur

The rod and spur or cordon system is often used for indoor grapes in glasshouses or conservatories, and for growing grapes against walls. It is commonplace in vineyards where the grapes are harvested mechanically.

This system trains one or two fruiting arms along a main wire, which can be low or high.

Bush

The bush system, a variation of which is known as gobelet, is often used in warmer vine-growing areas in southern France and Spain. Air circulation is poor through the bush so it is less likely to be used in rainy areas or ones with spring frosts. The vines are free standing.

The winemaker's year

Growing grapes and making wine is a simple process which follows the rhythms and cadences of the seasons – each winegrowing area will have its own timetable depending on its climate, so the dates might vary. But essentially, the pattern and tempo for every grower will be similar.

In fact, it all depends where you are in the world. In the southern hemisphere harvesting is likely to begin in February; in the north it is more likely to be September.

JANUARY
If left to their own devices vines will continue to grow. However, winemakers like to control them and give the vine a vigorous pruning – 95% of growth needs to be cut away. In the winery, barrels of wines made from last year's grapes will be carefully watched and checked for infection. Older vintages will often be bottled and made ready for sale.

▲ **Cold weather is a time of dormancy in the vineyard.**
(Burgundy Tourism)

◄ **Once pruned, cuttings will often be burnt.** (Burgundy Tourism)

FEBRUARY

Pruning continues – and cuttings will often be taken, grafted on to a root stock and kept in a greenhouse. Commercial vines are usually 10 to 30 years old so they will need replacing periodically. Now is the time to start to rack newly made wine. Most winemakers separate the clearing wine from the dead yeast and other proteins which make up the sediment, known as the lees, in the barrel.

MARCH

The sun is getting higher and the ground warmer. Sap will be rising and buds will be bursting. Now is the time to aerate the vineyard's soil, so it's time to get the tractor out. And the taking of cuttings is likely to be finished. The wine in the winery will begin its second fermentation.

APRIL

Ploughing in the vineyard continues. One-year-old cuttings will be planted out into freshly prepared ground. A weather eye will be kept on the thermometer. Frosts are still a possibility. The earth mounded up around the foot of the vine to protect it from frost will be removed, a process known as débuttage.

▲ **Newly grafted vines.** (Burgundy Tourism)

MAY

Ne'er cast a clout until May is out. Severe frosts can still happen, and in some vineyards stoves and heaters will be placed among the vines to ensure Jack Frost doesn't kill the new season's growth. The shoots will be culled, with the best

▼ **Working the soil with a horse-drawn plough.** (Burgundy Tourism)

▲ **Relevage – tieing up of new shoots.** (Burgundy Tourism)

tied on to the wires. The tieing of the shoots, a process known as relevage, allows light to get into the plants and makes it easier for tractors to pass along the row.

▼ **Winemakers like long periods of warm sun during the harvest season.** (Burgundy Tourism)

JUNE

The relevage continues and the branches are now tied to the horizontal wires. Flaming June brings soaring temperatures. The growing vines need warm weather if the flowers are to thrive and prosper. Depending on the temperature, flowers will start to appear.

JULY

A multitude of bugs appear as the days get warmer and longer. It is time to go on the offensive against them and also any weeds growing at the base of the vine. The shoot tips of the vine will be trimmed to divert the plant's energy into the grapes. Growers may remove some bunches of immature grapes to restrict output and improve quality.

AUGUST

It is one of the quietest parts of the winemaker's year. Thoughts begin to turn to the harvest. Equipment in the winery has to be checked. Black grapes will start to turn from green to their final colour. The grapes start to swell and are seemingly bursting with sweet energy.

SEPTEMBER

Picking is likely to begin; the winery will be cleaned and ready for action. The winemaker will be hoping for long, warm, dry

▶ **Once harvested, the grapes need to be gently but firmly crushed.** (Yalumba Wine Company)

days, with lots of sunshine. The grapes are regularly tested to check on their sugar quality. Once picked, the grapes will be crushed and the juice put into a fermenter.

OCTOBER

The new wine will be fermenting. But last year's wine is not forgotten and it will be racked again. Pressed grape skins can be used as a fertiliser on the land. Ageing and unproductive vines will be dug up and the ground readied for replacements. As the days get colder and the frosts arrives the leaves fall off the vines.

NOVEMBER

Out comes the plough and the earth will be broken up. Vines will be earthed up to protect them from the coming winter's frosts. The vines slip into a state of dormancy until warmed by sunshine in springtime. The newly fermented wine will be put into barrels – they'll have to be filled to the top and then frequently topped up as the liquid will evaporate through the oak casks.

▼ **Newly fermented wine is put into barrels.** (Burgundy Tourism)

DECEMBER

And so the year continues – the endless lifecycle of the winemaker means that hard pruning of the vines starts again, including the cutting off of unproductive canes and the branch on which the year's grapes were grown. It's time to taste the latest fermentations and ensure the barrels stay full.

Profile – Bothy Vineyard, where wine is art

'There's more philosophy in a bottle of wine than all the books ever written', proclaims the slogan on a t-shirt at the Bothy Vineyard in Oxfordshire.

Wine and art have long been associated. From the civilisations of ancient Greece and Rome, the early years of Christianity and on through the reformation, there have been close links between wine and art.

Wine has inspired artists, thinkers, writers and poets through the ages, and art and wine come together in close harmony in Oxfordshire's oldest vineyard. Now more than 36 years old, it began when Roger and Dorothea Fisher planted the first vines in 1978 and has since then seen Richard and Sian Liwicki take over the tradition.

Once a year, the grounds of Bothy Vineyard, Frilford Heath, Oxfordshire become home not just to three hectares of sustainable wine production and wildflower gardens, but 200 original sculptures, produced by over 30 local and UK-wide artists.

There is always much to see. It could be a rotating 15

◀ ▲ ▼ **Once a year, art and wine come together with a sculpture display at the Both Vineyard.** (Tim Hampson)

▲ **A stainless steel yacht sways and reflects the colours of Oxfordshire.** (Tim Hampson)

foot stainless steel yacht, a blue Neolithic Egyptian goddess and a life-sized horse gambolling among the wildflowers and budding vines. The sculptures are as diverse as the varieties of wine which can be made from grapes. Sculptures made from glass, bronze, marble and stone, wire-mesh and composites can all be found.

More than 50 sculptures can even be found in the winery's fermentation room. Here, next to a grape press and storage vessels, while yeast does its own work creating fine wines from grapes grown and picked barely metres away, are artistic creations of a human kind.

The winery's owners Sian and Richard Liwicki are committed to making wine from grapes cultivated in as environmentally-friendly a way as possible. In the vineyard, most of the work is done by hand – from pruning to winemaking. It's a labour-intensive process using the double Guyot system. The vines' fruiting arms are trained along wires, and require frequent pruning.

The vineyard seemingly has its own micro-climate and the warm sandy soil and long season make an invaluable contribution to the crispness and depth of the wines made here.

As much as possible is generated on site, even some of the electricity. Green compost grows between the vines, which will be harvested in the autumn and used to breathe life back into the hard-working soil.

The goodness from the compost feeds the nine varieties of early-ripening German red and white grape varieties which are used to make more than 7,000 bottles of crisp, aromatic rosé, sparkling, red and dry white wines annually.

Quality and not quantity is the order of the day. One good grape suitable for pressing is better than using those which will 'just about do'. The vines are hard pruned and the grapes carefully selected so that only the very best are used. This is true artisanal winemaking. Volumes are low, the output is sustainable, the carbon footprint is small and most of the wine is sold direct from the winery.

And we can all drink to that.

Bothy Vineyard

Frilford Heath, Abingdon, Oxfordshire OX13 6QW.

www.bothyvineyard.co.uk

▼ **Sculptures in the fermentation room.** (Tim Hampson)

Profile – Domaine de Bellevue

Wherever you look, vineyards. Welcome to Bordeaux, and the Domaine de Bellevue, Langoiran.

Located to the south-east of Bordeaux, on the right bank of the Garonne river, Bellevue commands a fine view over the town and is close to the town's limestone-built 12th-century medieval castle.

The rock for the castle and most of the town's buildings is hewn from the ground the vineyard stands on, and its large, cool cellar used to be a quarry. Today, it is home to oak barrels of ageing wine. The conditions are perfect.

Jean-Francois Boras is the co-proprietor and winemaker at Bellevue. It is clearly a task he adores. He is not a winemaker with a proud lineage going back several generations. Instead he is one of France's new generation of winemakers, and has only been making wine since 2002.

As a teenager in the 1970s he had the dream of owning his own small vineyard, but it took another 30 years or so for the fantasy to become a reality.

The land he bought for his vineyard fell into disuse in 1961, the year of his birth. And for 40 years, the grounds of this once

▲ **Jean-Francoise Boras gave up a career as an international consultant to become a winemaker.** (Cath Harries)

▼ **Almost as far as the eye can see, vines are growing.**
(Cath Harries)

▲ **Jean-Fancoise Boras says his wine is born from the soil.**
(Cath Harries)

thriving vineyard lay unused and overgrown and the house and winery fell into disrepair.

After careers in the French navy and as an international business consultant, Jean-Francois knew that time was running out for him to own a vineyard. So while still working as a consultant, he searched for some land to buy.

Finally, in 1999 he found the rundown and dilapidated four-hectare Bellevue. After months of tortuous and difficult negotiations to buy the land, the hard work to clear the ground and replant it began.

Making wine is like being an artist, says Jean-Francois. And his palette begins with the terroir – geology, geography and climate – on which his mix of Merlot and Cabernet grapes grow. The earth, together with the grapes and his skills as a winemaker, are able to create moments of 'magic and extraordinary moments of shared pleasure', wherever on the planet the wine is drunk, he says.

Jean-Francois says: 'Wine is born from the soil, and draws on all the elements – earth, water, air and fire, which represents yeast and fermentation. But there is a fifth element involved and that is a person, the winemaker.'

Clearly, passion and artistry are not enough to make good wine, so Jean-Francois enrolled at a local school for oenology. One day his professor, Kees van Leewen, visited the vineyard

and told him the soil at Bellevue was similar to some of the great wine chateaux around St Emilion.

He planted only 3.3 hectares of the south-west-facing vineyard, keen to leave margins of land where other wildlife could thrive, though he is not too keen on the small deer that live on the land, as they enjoy eating the buds on the vines.

He chose to plant a mixture of Merlot and Cabernet grapes, but unusually only made 35% of the 6,700 vines planted Merlot, saying that the preponderance of Cabernet would enable him to create a wine with freshness, elegance and the ability to age and mature.

Careful analysis of the terroir helped him decide the plots where each grape variety would be planted and he was thrilled to discover that his scientific planting matched that of the previous users of the land some four decades earlier.

He believes that he is the custodian of his land, and that it is important for him to leave it in a better condition than when he took it on.

His business philosophy isn't based on the constant need to increase profits and output from his land. He prefers quality to quantity, which means the ground and environment must be carefully nurtured and not destroyed through the overuse of fertilisers and pesticides. He wants to work in harmony with the land and believes some organic growers use too much permitted copper and sulphur treatments on their vines.

It wasn't easy at first, and the money needed for investment was tight. He was pleased with the wines made in 2005 and 2006, but unhappy with the 2007 crop, and his money was running out. His dreams of producing a great wine from the unique terroir of his land were becoming as stony as the land itself.

So in 2007, Jean-Francois decided he needed some help and decided to place a small advertisement in the *International Herald Tribune* seeking a business partner for his project to revitalise the vineyard.

By chance, the advertisement was seen by British entrepreneur Tim Griffiths, while on a skiing holiday, who pocketed the advertisement. Some weeks later he came across the advertisement again, and on a whim decided to contact Jean-Francois. The pair met and while drinking a bottle of one of Jean-Francois' first wines, vintage 2005, agreed to go into business together.

Their business model is unusual: rather than sell the wine on the open market, the pair decided to form an exclusive club, Le Grand Société, with members receiving an annual allocation of 36 bottles of wine. In many ways it is the ultimate networking opportunity, with Tim drawing on his years of business contacts in the quest to get people to join the club. And it seems to have worked, as now Bellevue has raised the capital needed to secure its future.

The deep, cool cellars have been cleared of 40 years of debris and are now home not just to the winery and barrels, but also the site of the club's annual dinner, which members

travel to from all over the world to celebrate the new harvest. Indeed, it's not unusual for some members to arrive by private helicopter.

In the 18th century, a previous owner of the land had also been a naval officer, and this is celebrated in Bellevue's coat of arms, which is displayed inside the Bellevue's cellars. One cellar is known as Paradise and behind its locked gates are kept bottles of the wine, gently slumbering. It is a perfect place to sample the wine, which Jean-Francois carefully draws from a barrel using a long pipette.

Clearly the entente cordiale between Jean-Francois and Tim is as successful as the blend of the Merlot and Cabernet grapes used to make the wine – each brings something else to the glass. Like the greatest blends the sum of the parts is greater than the whole.

Science and inspiration, passion and skill and business acumen and a dream have come together to create an environment for making great wines. 'Wine is a civiliser, it brings people together and that is what Le Grand Société is all about,' says Jean-Francois.

▲ **Good wine needs careful ageing in a cool, quiet cellar before it can be bottled.** (Cath Harries)

▼ **Behind a locked gate is a cellar calle Paradise.** (Cath Harries)

◢ **Each barrel will develop its own personality. Sampling is an essential job for the winemaker.** (Cath Harries)

Artisanal winemaking – Pierre de Lune

Château Pierre de Lune – the moonstone – vineyard is small by St Emilion standards, being only one hectare in size.

The grapes are tended by Tony Ballu and his wife Véronique, who also looks after their home which is a friendly, intimate guest house.

The Ballus bought the land and old stone-built farmhouse in 1999. It is unusual for the area, in that it is embraced by a large tree-shaded glade. Most of the area around St Emilion is a seemingly endless monoculture of massed ranks of vines. The Ballus' wood is a welcome green lung, where bees buzz and birds sing, which offers much needed shade and cool on hot summer days.

Tony, who was born in the Champagne region, is no stranger to making good wines as his day job is at the 20-hectare Château Clos Fourtet, close to the heart of the village of St Emilion, right on top of the limestone plateau, where he makes some classic Premier Grand Cru Classé B Bordeaux wines.

Production at the Pierre de Lune vineyard is small by comparison with most wineries in the area, as they only make 3,000 bottles a year. They could make more but prefer to keep production low. This is true artisan winemaking.

The 6,000 vines are grown using the Guyot system on a mixture of sand and gravel, and comprise 90% Merlot and 10% Cabernet Sauvignon grapes. As much as possible is done by hand, with the vines pruned to only six or seven stems. And as the summer sun gets higher and hotter the vine leaves are pruned back to expose the ripening grapes to more of the sunshine.

Fermentation takes place in stainless steel tanks, in a small ground floor room under the bedrooms. The grape juice has a 30 day cuvaison, with daily pigeages to rouse the liquid. And there is just enough room for 20 barriques.

Once fermentation has finished the wine matures for part of the time in new oak barrels, then in used barrels, before careful blending (assemblage) takes place.

The moon is important at the vineyard as biodynamic principles are followed. This means most of the decisions taken on when to prune and harvest the vines follow lunar cycles. The link between the moon's natural cycles and the fertility and health of the land is not clearly understood or easily explained, but it is a technique more and more winemakers are adopting.

In French, the name Pierre de Lune means 'moonstone', a gemstone which is reputed to have, just like a glass of wine, healing properties. It is said to be a calming stone which can be very effective in soothing the emotions.

The moonstone has been used to make jewellery for centuries. As such, it was much admired by the Romans. The name explains, in part, the moon on the chateau's label. However, the moon on the label is actually a piece of furniture created by Tony's brother, a cabinetmaker of some skill. He constructed a large, near perfect globe, made from resin and mussel shells. One of only 15 made, it houses a beautiful drinks cabinet – and once the lid is removed, it reveals a space perfect for a bottle of the chateau's wine, a crystal decanter and some glasses. Mounted on a gimbal, it doesn't seem to matter which way the globe is pushed, the bottle stays upright.

'Art, craft, engineering and wine, all come together in one object,' says Véronique.

▼ Shaded by trees, the chateau's garden offers some relief from the sun. (Cath Harries)

▼ Growing grapes requires much care, attention, and special machinery. (Cath Harries)

Terroir

Grainy, gritty, granity, rocky and salty – these are words often used to describe the taste of a wine. Indeed the terms are really in vogue at the moment. But can the rocks in the soil impart flavours into growing grapes which end up in a bottle of wine? Some think so, but scientifically the jury is out on the effect of rock on the wine in your glass.

SO WHAT IS TERROIR?

Like many French words there is no precise translation into English. It is a word beloved of winemakers and connoisseurs, but what does it mean?

The answer has as much to do with the heart as the head. It has something to do with the terrain, where the vines are growing, but that is only part of the story.

Proponents say that climate, soil, subsoil, topography – altitude, slope and orientation – must all be taken into account. The climate is also important: sunshine, rainfall and seasonal variations of temperature all have an influence on the taste of a wine.

To many winemakers terroir is an article of faith. In France, for instance, the Appellation Contrôlée system is based on it. The climate and geology of a region, and even the slope of a precarious vineyard perched on the side of a hill, all influence the character of wine in a bottle.

The Austrian winemaker Davis Weszeli has his own take on terroir. He calls it terrafactum. This means that the place, the vineyard itself, with its tremendous biological diversity, is crucial to his winemaking – 'because that is where the true character of the wine is formed'.

The vineyards of Weingut Weszeli winery are situated around the town of Langenlois, Austria, in an area famed

⚐ **A display shows the six different terroirs at the Weingut Weszeli vineyard.** (Cath Harries)

▲ **The rocky nature of the terroir at the Yalumba winery in Australia is evident.** (Australian Wine)

▶ **Davis Weszeli says that terroir helps form the true character of the wine.** (Weingut Weszeli)

for its wine production. And Weszeli believes that the terroir of each of his plots produces wines with different characteristics.

On several small plots comprising in total 30 hectares, Grüner Veltliner and Riesling grapes are grown. Each year he makes a number of single varietal wines using grapes only from each plot. Each is different with the vines growing in different types of rock formation, and he says this profoundly influences the taste of each wine.

He has produced a display which shows the different rock

formation for each of the plots. And he delights in describing the different tastes of each wine, which he believes are influenced by the microclimate of each site and differences in the plots' soil and rock composition.

It is as if the character of the six wines shown on his display really are set in stone.

STEINHAUS

Grapes for Steinhaus come from a south-facing slope to the west of Langenlois. In the sun-drenched vineyard, the ground is covered by many loose stones storing the heat of the day and giving it off far into the night.

As a result, the grapes mature evenly so that the wine takes on a 'playful elegance'. The topsoil is a thin sandy clay and the 30- to 40-year-old vines develop deep roots down into the rock.

In the gneiss layer below, calcareous marine sediments dating from the Tortonian period endow the grapes with a minerality rich in aromas.

PURUS

The grapes for the Grüner Veltliner Purus come from the Kittmannsberg, located in the south-west part of Langenlois.

Kittmannsberg is characterised by a particularly thick layer of loess. This soil dating from the ice age is very fine-grained and can store the heat of the sun well. 'It endows the wine with a rich body and soft acidity', says Weszeli.

He says the rock's lime content adds a succinct mineral note to the interplay of aromas.

SCHENKENBICHL

The Schenkenbichl plot is located in the north-west part of Langenlois. This south-facing slope features three terraces, set in the very centre of the slope.

The climate is characterised by high temperatures. The steep slope's southern exposure and surrounding stone walls retain heat well after the sun has set. The grapes ripen approximately ten days earlier than at the other sites and they can mature until late autumn, so making wine which is particularly intense.

Weszeli says the wine is shaped by the differences between the three terraces. In the west, stony gneiss results in a distinct minerality while in the east, loess provides the wine with a creamy body. This gives the wine an intensively fruity note.

KAFERBERG

The Kaferberg vineyard lies at 300 metres above sea level on a south-east-facing slope to the north of Langenlois. Its loose topsoil allows the vines to develop deep roots. As the vineyard lies on a former sea coastline, the underground contains marine sediment from those times. This richness in lime and silicates endows the wine with an extraordinary acidity structure and elegant minerality.

STEINMASSL

The Steinmassl plot is positioned just above the Steinhaus on a south-east-facing slope. The granite rock soil with its high iron content forms a solid basis for the vine. Given the loose texture of the brown soil on top of it, the vines can develop deep roots and fully exploit the terroir's potential.

The orientation of the slope protects the vineyard and its flora and fauna against cold north winds. Jerusalem artichokes, buckwheat, cornflowers and broom flourish.

SEEBERG

The Seeberg vineyard lies on a steep south-facing slope to the west of the village of Zobing. The site is made up of six large terraces.

Cooler than other sites used by Weszeli, the temperature differences between day and night let the grapes ripen slowly. This gives the wine a profound fruity note. The ground contributes spicy and mineral notes as the roots extend deep into the highly weathered garnet schist where they find a reservoir of pure lime.

The vineyard is highly popular among green lizards. They take sunbaths on the hot stones and enjoy the abundant, varied food provided by shrubs and berries.

SCIENTIFIC REALISM

So does the rock into which the vines are growing have an influence on the wine? Is this where the art of winemaking and science divide?

Professor Alex Maltman of the Institute of Geography and Earth Sciences, University of Wales in Aberystwyth, has done a lot of research into terroir. In an academic paper he says vineyard geology is much mentioned as an important factor in giving a wine a particular character – 'helping endow a typicity'.

'But critical evaluation of its role shows that there is misunderstanding about the possible connections, resulting in its significance commonly being exaggerated.

'The physical setting of a vineyard, ultimately due to bedrock geology, certainly affects parameters such as airflow patterns, slope character, thermal properties and water availability, and these demonstrably influence vine growth and berry ripening.'

He says, 'It is conceivable that such physical factors ultimately influence the development of flavour in the ripening berries, and hence in some indirect and as yet unknown way, the character of the eventual wine.'

So does the rock on which grapes grow affect the taste of the wine in a bottle? It is a clash between winemaking romanticism based on experience and scientific realism.

Clearly the conversation over terroir is one that winemakers and scientists are going to enjoy having for many years to come – over a glass of wine of course.

Caps, corks and screws – the bottle top

Is there a better sound than a cork being pulled from a bottle of wine? It is unmistakable.

But the wine world has changed in recent years – for many the cork has been replaced by a plastic stopper, however, for most of us the screw cap is the usual style of bottle top.

Sound can be a bit like smell – and evoke great memories and herald the promise of a glass of good wine.

Love them or loathe them, the screw cap is now the most common wine bottle topping in the world. The cap might not be seen as sexy as a cork made from tree bark, or even be equal to the sound of a plastic stopper being pulled from a bottle.

And though some winemakers like the synthetic cork, they can be hard to pull out of the bottle and they are even harder to put back in, in the unlikely event that you don't drink all the wine from the bottle in one go.

But the screw-on top caps the cork in several ways. It is far better at being a barrier than a cork to stop wine being spoiled.

Romantic they might be, but the problem with cork is that it can host a nasty little bug – commonly known as TCA – which can taint and spoil wines. Indeed some wine tasters say up to five per cent of wines are tainted or 'corked' and therefore undrinkable.

And for better or for worse, cork makers were slow to respond to winemakers' demands for a more sterile bottle top.

But the cap still poses as many questions as it answers. For wines which are kept for ageing, the cork has many fans. The traditional cork has a wonderful ability to let the wine breathe – and oxidation is an important element in the transformation of an ageing wine.

Thus far, we just don't know how screw-capped wines will age. So if you are buying a wine for drinking today, then a screw cap is just right. According to one piece of research most wine is drunk within eight hours of buying it. If buying a wine for ageing, then a cork is probably better.

However, there is a rhapsody to the ritual of opening a cork-stopped bottle. The screw-cap might guarantee consistency, but sniffing one after opening a bottle doesn't seem quite as joyful as enjoying the fragrance of an aromatic, tannin-infused cork.

(Tim Hampson)

Celebrity wines

Grapes are the stars for many celebs and here are some who like to wine.

Celebrities and wine are always close to hand, well glass in hand in fact. And when it comes to A-listers you can be sure that some bubbly or other wine will never be far away.

It's not a new trend: way back in ancient Greek and Roman times, the celebs of the day – philosophers, politicians and celebrated warriors – often owned their own vineyard.

(Francis Ford Coppola Winery)

KANYE WEST

The controversial rap star Kanye West has his own winery, named Yeezus Juice after the rapper's sixth studio album. The brand's first release is a demi-sec blanc de blanc sparkling wine, a nod to the rapper's taste for sweeter-style wines.

(Kanye West Yeezus Juice)

FRANCIS FORD COPPOLA

One of the first of today's era of celebs to buy into the wine business was film-maker Francis Ford Coppola. The maker of the Godfather series is as passionate about wines as films. A Californian winemaker since 1975, a red blend of Zinfandel and Cabernet Sauvignon is said to be his best.

(Francis Ford Coppola Winery)

(Armand de Brignac)

JAY Z

Another rapper, Jay Z, recently bought Armand de Brignac Champagne for a reported £150m. The celebrity Champagne brand is usually referred to in rap lyrics as 'Ace of Spades' because of its logo, and bottles sell for £250 and up. Indeed, well-heeled celebs have forked out more than £100,000 for a 30 litre bottle of the fizz.

(Elvis Presley Graceland Cellars)

ELVIS PRESLEY

Elvis Presley might have left the building but his bouquet lives on in a wine. His estate launched an Elvis Presley Graceland Cellars' Blue Christmas Cabernet Sauvignon. Only 4,000 cases of the first vintage were put on sale in 2002. And after more than ten years of maturing, anything left now could be really rocking around the clock.

STING

The rock band Police's lead singer Sting and his wife Trudie Styler's 'Message in a Bottle' is a wine made from grapes grown on his 350 hectare acre Italian estate, Il Palagio. Bought in 1999 when it was in a state of disrepair, the estate is run on biodynamic principles. So rather than 'Walking on the Moon', he's following its phases.

(Sting)

GREG NORMAN

Australian golfer Greg Norman has wineries in both the US and Australia. His nickname throughout his golfing career was the Great White Shark so it is only appropriate that the wine label has an image of the fish. And clearly his wines are better than par as he has won many plaudits from wine experts.

GREG NORMAN ESTATES

(Greg Norman Estates)

Coupe stack theatre

A sense of theatre is an essential part of enjoying glasses of bubbly.

Pouring Champagne into a coupe, a stack of six glasses one metre high, has to be the most dramatic and decadent way to serve the drink.

The tower is built glass by glass. And then when the bottle is open, the bubbly is poured into the top glass. It is poured at a steady pace so that the bubbles cascade gently from glass to glass. And it is essential to stop pouring when the bottom glass is half full.

When the cascade has stopped, the top glass will be full. The top glass can then be carefully removed and the others follow one by one. Then the fun can begin.

The inspiration for the modern day coupe – which uses glasses specifically made so they can be built as a tower – was Sir Arthur Page, Chief Justice of Burma. He was introduced to the trick by the flamboyant Maharajah Cooch

Behar, who had a flair for outrageous parties.

Sir Arthur was given a stack of glasses on his retirement from his job in Burma. An old Page family photograph showed the stack being joyously used at a family gathering, by Sir Arthur's son Sir Arthur John Page.

Barny Macaulay, a great grandson of Sir Arthur, decided with his brother Ian that they would recreate the coupe.

But how would it be done? Sadly the original family coupe had long since disappeared – only the faded black and white photograph remained.

The brothers set about recreating a modern day version of the coupe. It involved a lot of travel and several designs and prototypes. It was a hard task as they had to open many bottles of Champagne in an effort to ensure that their design was right. But someone had to do it.

(All photos Cath Harries)

(Tim Hampson)

The world's largest winery

The wine world often reveres the small, boutique wineries, where the number of cases of wine produced in a year can be counted on the fingers of two hands.

If they used the same counting technique at E & J Gallo, each digit would have to represent 10 million cases of wine, that's 120,000,000 bottles. The annual output from the Californian winery is more than 80 million cases.

E&J. Gallo Winery

Established in 1933 and headquartered in Modesto, California, E & J Gallo Winery remains a privately-held company which produces more than 60 different wine brands.

The company owns ten wineries and over 20,000 acres of vineyards across the states of California and Washington. In addition, the company maintains contracts with growers around both states that assist with yearly supply.

Well it needs a lot of grapes – its largest winery in Livingstone, California can process 7,000 tons of grapes a day; big it is but workers are clearly proud of their winemaking skills and call it 'the world's largest boutique winery'.

The company was founded by two brothers, Ernest and Julio Gallo, who started a winery in Modesto, California, just as Prohibition was ending.

The pair come from a long line of Italian winemakers and grape-growers. At first they made their name by producing cheap, fortified wines such as Thunderbird. However, as California's reputation grew for producing fine wines, the company realised it would have to adapt its strategy.

Early in 2015 the company bought another Californian producer, J Vineyards & Winery, which produces a wide range of prized sparkling wines, Pinot Noir and Pinot Gris.

Some of the brands in Gallo's wine portfolio include Gallo Family Vineyards, Barefoot Cellars, Apothic, Louis M. Martini and MacMurray Estate Vineyards.

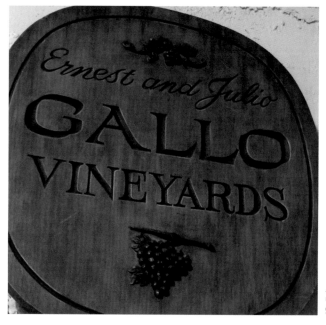

(Gallo)

(Milesti Mici)

The world's biggest wine cellar

So where is the world's biggest wine cellar – France, Italy, the USA or even China?

All good guesses, but Moldova? Most couldn't find the country on a map – but it is a very small country between Romania and Ukraine. Now how many could even find those two countries on a map of eastern Europe?

However, it is home to the State Enterprise Quality Wines Industrial Complex, known locally as the Mileştii Mici. Opened in 1969, and 80m underground, it comprises 120 miles of tunnels, two million bottles and barrels of wine. Most are red, some are white and there's a collection of sweet wines too.

It's regarded as the perfect place to store wines. And should you visit Moldova, tours of the underground wine complex can be arranged.

It's a strange and beautiful world.

The State Enterprise Quality Wines Industrial Complex 'Mileştii Mici'

Mileştii Mici Village, Ialoveni District, Republic of Moldova, MD-6819. www.moldova-wine.com.cn

Wine trick with a candle

Here's a trick to amaze your friends – could you fill an upside down glass with red wine without moving it?

EQUIPMENT NEEDED
- One glass
- One small candle/night light
- Plate
- Red wine

1 Light the candle, and drip some wax on to the centre of the plate. Fix the candle to this.

2 Pour approximately one third of a glass of wine on to the plate.

3 Put the glass over the wine.

4 When the wine rises up into the glass, hold it firmly and turn the plate over.

5 The wine is now in the glass, enjoy.

(All photos Cath Harries)

How to sabre a bottle of sparkling white wine

Health warning – *Be careful! Make sure the wine bottle is not pointing at someone when you try this. And take care when dealing with knives and broken glass...*

Celebration and commiseration are an important part of wine drinking.

One of the greatest pieces of wine theatre has to be opening a bottle of Champagne with a sabre, or sabrage as it is known. It is the stuff of legend and is said to have been a skill well-honed by Napoleon's cavalry officers, whether they had won or lost a battle.

There is even a world record for it, which is currently held by Julio Chang, who opened 55 bottles of Champagne with a sabre in one minute, at a wine festival in Sweden in March 2015, beating the record by seven.

You could do it at home if you want, and you do not have to have a sabre – a knife or spoon will do.

You should be able to do this trick with any well-made bottle of sparkling wine. Just make sure it is a heavy glass bottle – thin glass will not work – and it has to be a proper cork, it doesn't work with plastic stoppers.

1 Chill the sparkling wine in the fridge. Ideally you want it to be about 7°C. Don't try to cool the wine in an ice bucket, as this is unlikely to chill the neck.

2 Carefully remove the foil and wire. Don't shake the bottle as this might blow the cork out.

3 Next, find one of the two seams along the side of the bottle nearest the lip at the top of the bottle.

4 Hold the bottle at 45 degrees. Take care, it might be wet and slippy.

5 Now, imagine you are a French cavalryman celebrating a famous victory or even a defeat.

6 Harness your inner power and slide your sabre, knife or spoon along the seam and hit the glass ring at the top of the bottle.

7 If all goes well, the cork and the top of the bottle will fly away. And you should be left with a neatly cut bottle.

(All photos Cath Harries)

CHAPTER 3
WINE STYLES

(Cath Harries)

How to read a wine bottle label

Being able to interpret the label on a bottle of wine adds to the fun of enjoying what you pour into the glass.

These days many countries and regions such as the European Union have strict rules on what you can put not just in the bottle, but on the outside.

The rules don't always make for the most glamorous of reading, but a little understanding can help.

LABELLING RULES

Within Europe the front label should show:

- The country of origin of the wine.
- The category of wine – is it still, sparkling or fortified?
- The volume – in litres, centilitres or millilitres. Most wine in the UK is sold in 750ml bottles (75cl).
- The bottler.
- The alcoholic strength – alcohol by volume.

Also somewhere on the bottle there should be a lot number – this is an identification number assigned to a particular quantity or lot of material from a single manufacturer.

If the wine is a blend from more than one country, this should be made clear.

The bottler's details and its address should be shown. The term 'bottled for' should only be used if the company commissioning the bottling owned the wine at the time of bottling.

Optional information which should be on a label includes any trade mark or brand name, traditional terms, colour, vine variety and vintage. Producers can put on other information, but it shouldn't be misleading.

Some wines are designated as *Protected Designation of Origin (PDO)* or *Protected Geographical Indication (PGI)*.

PDO/PGI categories

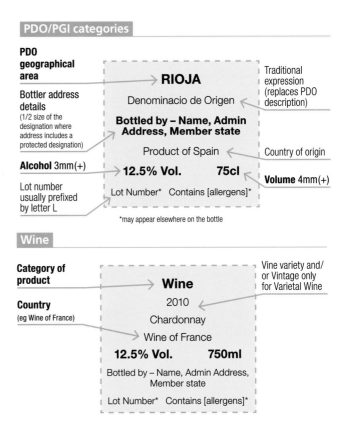

PDO geographical area →

Bottler address details
(1/2 size of the designation where address includes a protected designation)

Alcohol 3mm(+) →

Lot number usually prefixed by letter L

RIOJA

Denominacio de Origen ←

Bottled by – Name, Admin Address, Member state

Product of Spain ←

12.5% Vol.   **75cl**

Lot Number*   Contains [allergens]*

Traditional expression (replaces PDO description)

Country of origin

Volume 4mm(+)

*may appear elsewhere on the bottle

Wine

Category of product →

Country
(eg Wine of France)

Wine

2010

Chardonnay

Wine of France

12.5% Vol.   **750ml**

Bottled by – Name, Admin Address, Member state

Lot Number*   Contains [allergens]*

Vine variety and/or Vintage only for Varietal Wine

A **PDO** is a wine which is produced, processed and prepared within a particular geographical area. If it is labelled as English wine, it means the grapes can be of many varieties but all must be grown in England.

A PDO could refer to a named area or a specific place such as Champagne, and is similar to terms which are still in use such as Appellation Contrôlée in France and Prädikatswein in Germany. And importantly, it must have some attributes which are influenced by its environment.

A **PGI** is slightly less restrictive and is defined as the name of a region, a specific place or a country used to describe a wine.

A PGI wine should possess a specific quality, reputation or other characteristics attributable to the geographical origin. At least 85% of the grapes used for its production must have come from that area and be of the Vitis vinifera genus, or a cross of Vitis vinifera and another genus of Vitis.

A PGI could include a Vin de Pays in France or a Landswein from Germany.

There are also rules on the use of descriptors such as dry, medium dry, medium, medium sweet and sweet. Wines so named must fall within a certain range of residual sugar in grams per litre.

There are limitations too on the use of some terms – wines labelled Château should come from France or Luxembourg. Reserva is a term which can only be used by producers in Spain and Chile.

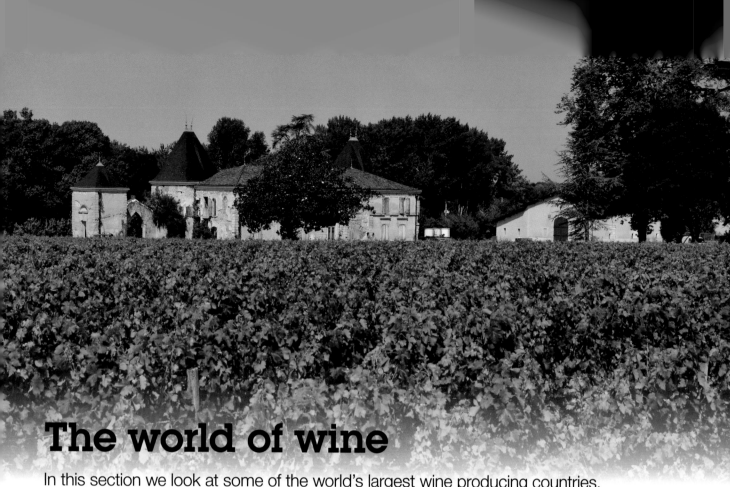

The world of wine

In this section we look at some of the world's largest wine producing countries.

Grapes for winemaking are grown in many countries both in the Old World and the New. The top 12 producing countries account for 65% of this growing area and the three largest producers – Italy, Spain and France – are responsible for nearly one in two bottles of wine drunk.

Despite this lead by European countries, New World producers Chile, Australia, New Zealand, South Africa and USA have enjoyed rapid growth, with combined volume production rising by 370% between 1995 and 2013.

The Old World is broadly defined by appellations, rules and restrictions, and relatively small vineyards. The brave New World wine producing countries don't really allow themselves to be constrained in that way. They are big, brash and happen to make some fantastic wines.

FRANCE

Top French wine regions

- Alsace
- Beaujolais
- Bordeaux
- Burgundy
- Champagne
- Côtes du Rhône
- Jura
- Languedoc
- Loire Valley
- Médoc
- Provence

At times it seems like the whole of France is one vast vineyard. It has the richest wine heritage of any country, offering something for everyone, with grapes grown from Champagne in the north down to Provence on the shores of the Mediterranean and the foothills of the Pyrenees.

The country has just about every grape-growing climate. And the years of growing have seen a process of natural selection, with different grape varieties prospering in different regions.

▲ **Much of France seems given over to the growing of vines.** (Cath Harries)

▼ **Rules in France often restrict the volume of grapes which can be harvested from any vineyard.** (Cath Harries)

It is home to most of the world's classic wine styles. The country has also adopted a complicated classification system called Appellation Contrôlée, a way of identifying where a wine has been made. For most French wines location, location, location is the important thing, but there will also be regulations about grape varieties. In Burgundy an appellation can apply to a particular field just a few hectares in size. In Bordeaux it can cover a village, as with St Emilion.

Each appellation has its own unique set of rules defining the land and grapes which can be used. Plant the wrong grapes and you don't get the appellation. The alcoholic strength is specified, as is the yield of juice per hectare of grapes planted. Make too much juice and you don't get the appellation.

The number of vines planted per hectare is also specified, as is the method of pruning. New World winegrowers rarely shackle themselves with such restrictions on production. The winemaking process is also defined and permits or prohibits such practices as adding sugar, acidifying or de-acidifying.

And finally, to achieve the appellation the wines have to go through a tasting panel. If the tasters don't like it, it doesn't get the appellation.

GERMANY

The German wine industry is defined by its northerly location, the steepness of many of its vineyards and the sweetness of its wines. It also has some of the most convoluted wine labels in the world.

▲ **As the grapes ripen, autumn mist hangs over the river Moselle in Germany.** (Hans Peter Mertin)

▼ **The Rhine runs through some of Germany's most productive vineyards** (Dietmae Scherf, Deutsche Zentrale für Tourismus)

The country's wine industry is spread out over 13 regions, each region having its own soil quality and topography. The Rhine and Mosel are probably the best known.

Because of Germany's mild climate, grapes take longer to ripen than in more southerly countries. The longer grapes stay on the vine, the more aroma and flavour they develop.

German winemakers can add sugar to their wines, which has given the country an unfair reputation of making very sweet wines. Riesling is probably the country's best known grape.

Like any wine label, you'll find the name of the producer, the vintage, the region, and sometimes the name of the grape on a German wine label. It is just a shame most are incomprehensible.

Most German wines are white. The quality of German wine is determined by the ripeness/sweetness of the grapes at harvest. The riper the grapes, the sweeter they are and thus the higher amount of natural sugar in the juice.

Qualitätswein mit Prädikat or Prädikatswein denotes the highest quality of German wine. It must have been made from fully ripened grapes and must be produced exclusively from grapes grown in one of the 13 wine regions. These wines are completely natural – the winemaker may not add any additional ingredients, such as sugar or yeast, to the grape juice.

AUSTRIA

In the eastern highlands of Austria, they say gold can be found and it is liquid. The country's wine production might not be huge, but its winemakers prefer quality to quantity.

Small is indeed beautiful. What sets Austria apart is the fragmented nature of its wine industry. Thousands of small family-run vineyards, often in inhospitable rocky locations,

▲ **Most German wines are white, but they make fine rosés and reds too.** (Ernst Wrba, Deutsche Zentrale für Tourismus)

▼ **In Austria, steep but productive vineyards line the Wachau valley.** (Austrian Tourist Board)

▲ **Many of Austria's vineyards are very old and family owned.**
(Austrian Tourist Board)

▲ **Winter frost has kissed the vineyards near Gols.**
(Austrian Tourist Board)

create wines mainly from indigenous grape varieties. Many of the country's vineyards are generations old and for hundreds of years the families that have tended them have followed the ups and downs of the seasons.

In Austria there are 35 officially approved grape varieties – 22

white and 13 red. Chief among them is Grüner Veltliner, whose spiritual home is Vienna and the adjoining Weinviertel region. However, in recent years more red grape varieties are being grown.

Most Austrian wines are white. Many of them might seem similar in style to German wines, but broadly they have will more body and alcohol than their neighbour. The country's cool climate and often stony terroir has a profound effect on the wines produced.

The country is renowned for its sweet wines, including a style known as Strohwein. Bunches of grapes are laid out on beds of straw in lofts and barns during the winter months. This process leads to the fruit taking on extra sweetness.

◀ **Harvesting grapes in southern Styria is often done by hand.**
(Austrian Tourist Board)

▼ **Wine slowly and gently matures in a cellar in Styria.**
(Austrian Tourist Board)

▶ **Italy competes with France for being the biggest producer of wine in the world.** (Cath Harries)

ITALY

Top Italian wines

- Alto Adige
- Asti
- Chianti
- Chianti Classico
- Conegliano Valdobbiadene
- Montepulciano d'Abruzzo
- Piemonte
- Prosecco
- Soave
- Trentino

Italy has a rich vinicultural history, dating over two thousand years, which includes influences from the Greeks, Etruscans and Romans who all contributed to the development of Italy's wines. It is divided into 20 wine regions, with Tuscany and Umbria probably being the best known.

The country's Mediterranean sunshine, cool, mountain air currents and sea breezes make it a good place to grow vines; indeed every piece of open, rocky ground, however sheer, seems to be home to some vines.

Italy vies with France for being the biggest wine producer in the world, a mantle which is swapped between the two on a regular basis.

The top 10 denominations account for about half the total volume and value of wine produced in the country. The biggest by far is the sparkling favourite Prosecco, which has become the drink of choice for many people when celebrating.

Italy offers a larger, more diverse array of wine styles than almost any other nation, most of which are officially named, defined and protected under the Italian wine classification system. This is known as Denominazione di Origine Controllata (DOC) and it is similar to the French Appellation Contrôlée. It lists more than 900 different types of wine from more than 240 locations.

It is said that more than 1,000 different grape varieties are grown in Italy.

SPAIN

The rain in Spain really does fall on the plain, or more correctly an elevated plateau. Other than the coastal fringes very little of the country is at sea level. It is not uncommon to find vineyards at above 1,000m high.

Spain has a greater acreage of land planted for grapes than France or Italy, but its production is much lower. Traditionally Spanish growers have not planted vines as densely as in other parts of the word, hence the lower yields. However, Spanish growers are slowly starting to increase yields.

Rioja in northern Spain is the country's largest wine region, renowned for its red wine. The main grape in Rioja is Tempranillo, but the region's wine regulations permit another three varieties for reds — Garnacha, Graciano and Mazuelo — and red Rioja wine is typically a blend of two or more varieties.

Spain is also home to a sparkling white wine called Cava, which comes from Penedés in Catalonia, south of Barcelona.

Other wine regions in Spain include Ribera del Duero, Priorato and Toro, which are fast gaining a reputation for making full-bodied reds.

The best Spanish whites are said to be made from the Verdejo grape.

Spanish winemakers are continuing to develop their own appellation called Denominacion de Origen. Exceptional vintages are called Gran Reserva, and must be aged in wood for two (or three) years followed by three (or two) years in bottle. White and rosé versions are aged for four years, of which six months must be in oak.

PORTUGAL

It is impossible to write anything about the Portuguese wine industry without mentioning port, a 19th century creation.

Portugal's wine was already well regarded in Britain as various blockades following wars with France saw restrictions on wines being exported from there.

The remote Portuguese island colony of Madeira traded in

▲ Many of Portugal's winemakers do not know the name of the grape variety they grow. (Wines of Portugal)

wine too. It developed a sweet wine, with swathes of caramel caused by the heat of long sea voyages. Today this is done using a process known as estufagem, a baking process which is supposed to replicate the effects of a barrel being shipped in the hot hold of a ship, sailing the high seas.

▼ Britain's various wars with France helped to make Portuguese wine popular in England. (Wines of Portugal)

Estufagem caramelises the sugar in the wines and oxidises it, giving the wine a distinctive taste almost like burnt butterscotch.

The Douro region is by far the most significant for the production of fine wines.

Portugal is also known for its rosé wines, such as Mateus, though the country seems to have missed out on the current trend for people to drink rosé wines, which today are primarily made in the New World.

The country has introduced its own appellation system, but it has to be said there are many growers making wines who haven't the faintest idea of the grape variety they are using.

UNITED STATES OF AMERICA

Grapes are grown in all 50 US states, but California accounts for most of it, as it is where 90% of the country's wine is made. Washington, Oregon and New York are the next biggest producers. The country has a lot of wineries too, more than 8,000.

Wine has been produced in the US since the early 17th century, when Europeans started to colonise it, using indigenous grape varieties. However, the early experiments were not too successful as the native species produced wines which matched neither the style nor the quality to which the first settlers were accustomed. European varieties were introduced in the mid-1650s, but they soon succumbed to the resident phylloxera. It took a couple of hundred years for vine breeding and grafting to be refined to produced strong, healthy vines suitable for wine production.

The modern industry began to take off in the 1970s and there are now about 200 areas of appellation. Today the US is the world's fourth-biggest wine-producing nation – behind France, Italy and Spain.

California is home to some of the world's biggest wineries, such as Gallo, but it also hosts some forward-thinking boutique wineries, whose wines sell for sky-high prices. The state's first vineyards were planted by Spanish monks and missionaries, who arrived via Mexico.

The main grape varieties grown in California are Cabernet Sauvignon and Chardonnay. A wide range of traditional European (Vitis vinifera) vines also flourish, grafted to hardy, phylloxera-resistant American roots. Not as well known are American/European hybrids, producing wines mainly for local consumption.

Soils and climates vary substantially throughout the state. Generally, the cooler regions closer to the coast are better suited to Pinot Noir and Chardonnay, while in the hotter inland regions Cabernet Sauvignon vines are grown. Zinfandel grows in many parts of the state and produces some outstanding wines.

▲ **California's first vineyards were planted by Spanish monks and missionaries.** (Californian Wine Institute)

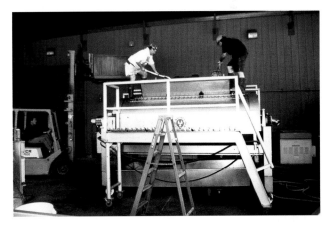

▲ **California accounts for 90 per cent of the wine made in the USA.** (Californian Wine Institute))

▼ **The USA now has more than 8,000 wineries, from the vast to some inspirational boutique winemakers.** (Californian Wine Institute)

▼ **Red grapes prosper in the hotter part of California and are much sought after.** (Californian Wine Institute)

CHILE

They like to think big in Chile. The wine industry has set itself the ambitious target of being the number one producer of premium, sustainable, and diverse wines of the New World by 2020. Only time will tell if they achieve that ambition, but in the meantime they make some fine wines.

The country has 14 distinctive wine regions, with different soils and climates, which makes it perfect for growing a large range of grape varieties.

It is best known for growing Cabernet Sauvignon, Carménère, Sauvignon Blanc, Syrah and Pinot Noir grapes.

◄ **Chile's unashamed ambition is to make the best wine in the world.** (Cath Harries)

Cabernet Sauvignon is the most grown grape, making up 35% of the country's winemaking grapes. No other country in the world has more Cabernet Sauvignon planted than Chile. The country is fast gaining a reputation for making single varietal grape wines.

Carménère is becoming regarded as Chile's signature grape. A red varietal, it disappeared from French vineyards in the mid-19th century, phylloxera probably seeing it off. It reappeared among Chile's Merlot vines a hundred years later.

In recent years, Chile's exports of Sauvignon Blanc have grown and grown with most of the output heading to the United Kingdom.

ARGENTINA

Red meat and wines, red is certainly the signature colour of Argentina.

Malbec is probably the country's best known grape and is used in its most sought-after wines. However, a greater acreage is given over to Criolla Grande, which is used in many of the country's cheap and cheerful table wines for easy drinking.

Criolla Grande is grown in the region of Mendoza, under the shadow of the Andes, and it comes with pink skin. The wine

▼ **In Argentina, a gaucho rides through a vineyard.**
(Wines of Argentina)

▲ **Malbec is Argentina's best-known grape variety.**

(Wines of Argentina)

▶ **The very best grapes are picked by hand, not machine.**

(Wines of Argentina)

made from it is often sold locally in cardboard cartons. It is not a grape which has been used to make wines for laying down. It is recommended to be consumed early on, compared to other wines which improve when aged.

The country's hot climate makes it more suitable for red varieties, but some white grapes are grown including Torrontés and Chardonnay. However, as many more vineyards are being planted, it is likely that the more southerly ones, heading towards the place where penguins live, will be for white grapes.

Summer hailstones are a challenge to growers, and the fear of having a crop destroyed by a deluge of ice balls sees many growers harvesting grapes early.

AUSTRALIA

Most European wine countries have a wine heritage which stretches back hundreds of years. Australia's wine industry is 200 years young and in that time it has grown from a few vines to one of the top 10 producers in the world.

Vines arrived with the first European settlers in 1788 and from small beginnings, some vines growing in the Governor's garden in Sydney, the country now has more than 60 winegrowing areas. Most grapes are grown in the cooler south-east, but it is not unusual to find a working, productive vineyard almost anywhere in the country. Even Alice Springs, in the bone dry red centre of the country, has its own small vineyard.

Almost every climate and soil type can be experienced in Australia, which means that winemakers can produce all the major wine styles – red, white, fortified and sparkling.

▲ **Australian producers make an astonishing variety of wines.**
(Cath Harries)

◀ **A cooper has to char the inside of a barrel, which helps bend the staves to shape.** (Yalumba)

The country also has some of the oldest grapes in the world: the early imports were pre-phylloxera and the bugs which destroyed Europe's vine heritage have not wreaked havoc here, though there are active pockets of it in some areas.

More than 100 different grape varieties are grown and Australia is starting to explore which grape varieties grow best in each area, from Cabernet Sauvignon in Coonawarra to Riesling in Clare Valley to Shiraz from the Barossa Valley.

Today, Australia exports its wines to more than 100 countries.

▶ **Australian has some of the oldest grapes in the world.**
(Yalumba)

▼ **More than 100 grape varieties are grown in Australia.** (Yalumba)

▶ **A snow-covered New Zealand vineyard in winter's grip.**
(Ballochdale)

NEW ZEALAND

New Zealand might be in the same hemisphere as Australia, but the conditions for growing vines are quite different.

Grapes are grown from the sub-tropical Northland down to the world's most southerly grape-growing region, Central Otago. The vineyards are all within 80 miles of the coast and benefit from long sunshine hours and cooling winds from the sea at night. This means the grapes have a long ripening period, which allows flavour development while retaining a vibrant level of acidity.

The country's first vineyard was established in 1850 at Hawke's Bay by Roman Catholic missionaries.

It was Sauvignon Blanc that first brought the country to the attention of the wine world, but today Bordeaux-style blends and Syrah grow in Hawke's Bay and further north, while Pinot Noir and Riesling are grown in the southerly regions. The climate is ideal for these grapes which require a long ripening period.

▼ **Grape picking his hard, repetitive work when carried out by hand.** (WM Destiny Bay Wines)

(Palliser)

When it comes to maturing wines, New Zealand winemakers prefer steel to wood, using technology derived from the milk industry. This, according to many wine critics, is why the country's wines have such crisp, clean tastes.

SOUTH AFRICA

The first Dutch settlers to South Africa in 1655 brought vines with them. Traders rather than farmers, they understood the value of grapes as a commercial commodity but didn't have the skills for the vines to flourish.

The first grapes were pressed in 1659, but not until the arrival of the French Huguenots around 1680, with their tradition of making wine, did winemaking really take hold.

Vine-growing takes place predominantly in the Western Cape Province, in an area with a mild Mediterranean climate. The vines are cooled by breezes from the cold Benguela current that flows northwards from Antarctica into the Atlantic. Growing also takes place in the Northern Cape Province alongside the Orange River and a small amount in the province of KwaZulu-Natal.

The country's signature variety is Pinotage, a crossing of Pinot Noir and Cinsault. It is a variety rarely found anywhere else in the world. Other varieties planted include Shiraz, Cabernet Sauvignon and Merlot. The last two are often found together in a Bordeaux-style blend. Chenin Blanc is the country's most-planted grape, and South African Chardonnay and Sauvignon Blanc have become popular internationally in recent years.

CHINA

Vines are grown in China? You bet, and lots of them. Recently, China has overtaken France as the country with the second largest area under vines.

Wine has been made in China for thousands of years, but its modern industry is still relatively young. It has grown rapidly in recent years, with the number of wineries more than doubling over the past decade, and its volume of production easily put it into the world's top 10 producing nations.

By 2020 it is predicted that 70,000 hectares will be growing wine in ten different regions. There are currently about 100 wineries and it is thought that this number will soon double.

There are four prime vineyard regions, the biggest in the north-west Xinjiang, which accounts for 40% of production. Wine produced here is said to be similar in character to those from Argentina. A fast-growing region is the Loess Plateau, at 800 to 1,200 metres high, it is located on a similar latitude to Bordeaux and Cabernet Sauvignon grapes are grown. In northern provinces like Ningxia, Shanxi or Xinjiang, summers are conveniently warm and dry, but in autumn the temperatures plummet very quickly and growers have to bury their vines to protect them.

It is said that once China's winemakers master the art and skill of maturing wine, the country will experience its second red revolution.

As yet very little Chinese wine is exported, but given the size of its internal market that probably isn't giving any of the producers sleepless nights.

What's in a blend?

Wine is just made from grapes isn't it? Well yes, but the grapes in your wine bottle might come from different bunches or varieties.

(Cath Harries)

Many wines are made from what's called a single varietal – but there are also many wines which are blends of different varieties.

Blended wines are wines made from two or more grape varieties. If an EU wine contains less than 85% (in the New World 75%) of the predominant grape variety then it is technically a blended wine.

And indeed across the wine world blending is commonplace. The Australians are now past masters at it, which is why their wines are so reliably consistent.

Single varietal wines on a store's shelf will have labels indicating that they are made from grapes such as Malbec, Chardonnay or Pinot Grigio. Even some of these will be blends of a certain kind – for the wine may have been made from grapes from different parts of the vineyard, or from different regions in the same country, and in some cases even the same grape variety from different parts of the world.

At this point red and white wines can become a bit grey. But before anyone gets too sniffy about blends, just remember that some of the world's greatest wines are blends. Champagne is usually made from two or three different grape varieties, Châteauneuf-du-Pape is a blend and the melding of Cabernet Sauvignon and Merlot creates some of the world's greatest wines.

As already mentioned, in the US and Europe single varietal wines can include small amounts of other grapes, perhaps up to 25%, but in most cases it is likely to be less. But most blends are what they say they are – usually 40 to 50% of one grape varietal, and then a mix of a couple of other grapes.

One blended wine frequently found on sale is the Spanish Rioja. A typical Rioja will contain around 60% Tempranillo with other Spanish grapes making up the rest of the wine. In this case the name 'Rioja' therefore denotes a particular region rather than a grape.

In the same way, a red Bordeaux is commonly made from a blend of red grapes, the dominant one being Cabernet Sauvignon and the other Merlot. Similar blends are used in the New World.

Winemakers from the Rhône region in France blend up to 15 different grapes to make red and white wines of the highest quality. The main grapes in such a blend are likely to include Grenache, Syrah, Mourvèdre, Cinsault and Viognier.

Creating the blend is probably the most creative part of being a winemaker. It's a moment when all their olfactory and taste skills are needed. It's likely that the wine in every barrel will be rigorously tasted and considered, before the task of blending begins.

Blending adds complexity, aroma, colour and character to a wine. Within a winery wine is constantly being assessed. What is its finish? Is it big? Does it need something? Blending in no way means lower quality; if it did we'd never drink a glass of Rioja. And not many of us would say no to a glass of Burgundy.

This is the art of the winemaker – what will turn the unfinished painting intro a work of art?

The winemaker will think, does the base wine need something fresher, does it need to be matured in oak or mixed with a cocktail of different varietals? Typically a wine such as a Chardonnay will be made from blends of the same grape which have been stored in different containers – some in oak and some not – for different lengths of time.

At its best such a varietal is more than the sum of its parts, it's something even bigger. And there might be more than one grape variety in a blended wine, which when stored in oak vats or barrels brings new complexities of taste.

Of course, the French have transformed blending into an art form. The master blenders and their 'assemblage' skills are highly respected and much sought after.

But there are some grapes that just shun the company of others. One such is Pinot Noir which is rarely used in blends except for the making of Champagne.

VINTAGE BLENDS

A vintage wine blend is made of different grapes grown in the same year. One of the most complex is Châteauneuf-du-Pape, which will include more than 12 different grape varieties. Most are much simpler in construction – Chardonnay and Semillon or Cabernet and Shiraz, for example.

NON-VINTAGE BLENDS

Some blends are a meld of grapes grown in different years. The label will show that they are non-vintage and is unlikely to include a year. Port and Champagne are often constructed in this way. The skill of the blender is needed to balance the complexity of flavours and tannins.

Assemblage

Visitors to one of St Emilion's grandest winemakers can learn the art and craft of assemblage and design their own, unique classic wine, which they can take home and drink.

'You are building a dream,' says winemaker Pierre Dufourq at Château Fombrauge, the largest maker of Grand Cru Classé in St Emilion.

(Cath Harries)

With more than 60 hectares of vines growing, it features a complex tapestry of limestone and clay terroirs. It has the look and feel of a large traditional European winemaker, with its use of art, craft and science to make the wines.

But to this has been added modern technology, as Fombrauge uses drones to enable every square centimetre of the estate to be scrupulously monitored.

Fombrauge wines are typically a blend of 75% Merlot, 15% Cabernet Sauvignon and 10% Cabernet Franc. They are big and expressive wines. The grapes are fermented in temperature-controlled concrete vats and the wine is then matured in one of 600 oak barriques for around 15 months.

According to Pierre the wine is best when it has had at least five years of bottle ageing.

And that is where the skill of assemblage comes in, tasting samples of wines made from different grapes, evaluating their character and then blending two or three wines together.

Today's blend will comprise a mixture of only two grapes: Merlot and Cabernet Sauvignon. Both are young wines.

(Cath Harries)

'You have to be objective, and listen with your mouth,' says Pierre. 'You are trying to imagine the future and deciding how the wine will evolve. You want the blend to be bigger than the sum of the parts. One plus one should make three.'

Each wine is carefully nosed, sipped, tasted and evaluated.

'You are putting together a wine to be drunk at a big occasion,' says Pierre. 'This is not wine to be drunk as an aperitif, but wine for a memorable dinner in the company of friends and family.'

The Merlot is young, brash and loud and full of bold plum flavours. The Cabernet is somewhat restrained and more laid-back. It has hints of spice.

After evaluation a blend of 70% Merlot and 30% Cabernet is decided upon. The wines are poured into a container and a sample is taken and evaluated.

Once the taster is happy with the blend, sufficient quantities of the two base wines are mixed together and poured into a bottle.

The cork is then put into the bottle and it is labelled.

(All photos Cath Harries)

Red, white or rosé?

A little bit of knowledge can make reading a wine list much easier. Here's a brief guide to some wine styles and the grapes they are made from.

At its simplest there is white, red and rosé. Add to these sparkling, sweet and dessert wines and the task gets a little more complex.

Wines can be defined by grape variety, and you'd expect a Chardonnay to taste different from a Shiraz. But not all Chardonnay wines taste the same – so the classification only helps so far.

And then wines can be defined by region – all Riojas come from Spain, but not all Riojas are the same. Most are red, some are white; many are made using the Tempranillo grape, but other grape varieties or a mixture of them could be used too.

In France, wines are often defined by region and not the grape – for instance, Chablis is not a grape, it is a region, where the wine is made using Chardonnay grapes.

Red wines can be full, light or even medium. The full wines are big on tannins, are higher in alcohol and tend to be sipped and savoured rather than swallowed. Then there are the pink, rosé variants, and that's before we get to white. Some whites are dry, some fuller and sweeter, there are dessert wines and sparkling too. And of course some red wines can come with a bubble.

SOME COMMON WINE STYLES BY GRAPE VARIETY

Whites

Chardonnay – Possibly the most versatile wine style in the world. Its flavours and characteristics are influenced by

where it is grown and made. The flavour spectrum can range from apple and citrus to tropical. Often it has been barrelled in oak – this unveils butterscotch, honey and butter flavours. Yet if it has been matured in stainless steel it has fresh, mineral notes.

Chardonnay is widely grown in Burgundy, France and Australia.

Riesling – The wine which made New Zealand famous. Expect to find clean, crisp, apple flavours, or possibly some lemon citrus notes. There could be hints of mineral and salty notes. Good examples come from Alsace in France, Germany, New Zealand, Washington State, New York and Australia.

Pinot Gris – Its characteristics depend on where it comes from. In Italy (where it is called Pinot Grigio) it tends to be fresh and crisp. Richer versions come from the Americas, New Zealand and the Alsace region of France.

Sauvignon Blanc – Order a white wine from the Loire or Bordeaux and it is likely it will have been made from this grape, often blended with Semillon. The wine should be crisp and have a big floral aroma. It is a grape widely grown in the New World, where some variants are big and fulsome.

Reds

Cabernet Sauvignon – This is a fulsome grape, rich in tannin flavours. It is the grape of choice for people making wines to age. Wines made from it are full of dark fruit flavours, plums and blackcurrants. When aged in oak expect to find vanilla, chocolate, tobacco, even coffee. In Bordeaux it plays a major part in the greatest wines of the region. But it is also a handsome contributor to great wines from California, Australia and Chile.

Merlot – Listen to the sound of a blackbird singing in a Bordeaux vineyard and you get an idea of what the wine might taste like. It is a curious mixture of assertive boldness and mellow softness. It is often used in blends, especially with the tannin-rich Cabernet Sauvignon. New World variants from California or Chile are luscious and ripe and have a dark plum colour. European versions, especially from Bordeaux, are fresher with strawberry and raspberry flavours, and have a tantalising level of tannins.

Pinot Noir – A Bordeaux favourite, it makes some of the most famed single varietal wines in the world. Drink it young and it plays like gentle harp music, with a host of soft fruit raspberry

◀ **Botrytis, the so-called noble rot, produces fine sweet grapes.**
(Pegasus Bay Winery)

▲ Sauvignon Blanc grapes are successfully grown in New Zealand. (Palliser)

and strawberry flavours. As time goes by it adds a layer of earthy, almost burnt wood flavours. New World versions can have a rock and roll rhythm – bursting with big flavours and energy.

Shiraz – The grape's name almost sounds like its taste, spicy. Widely grown in the Rhone region of France (where it is known as Syrah), it adds great complexity to aged wines. When grown in Australia it adds a loud, bold contribution to a wine with notes of leather, blackcurrant and a mouth warming acid balance. In the US it seems the drink of choice with rich meaty barbecues. However, there are also lighter, more mellifluous variants.

Zinfandel – A Californian favourite. It produces big, spicy fruit flavours in red wines; a white variant is now often cited as being the first alcoholic drink for the state's teenagers. The white version is light and lacks the boldness of the red.

Rosés

Rosé wines are pink in colour and often medium-sweet, although some can also be very dry. They are usually made from black grapes, with the skin included for just the first few hours of the fermentation process to impart a small amount of colour to the wine. These are usually light, easy-drinking wines.

Some useful terms for describing wines

- ■ **Full red** – Think of a big Burgundy or Shiraz.
- ■ **Medium red** – Think of the Malbec grape, an easy-drinking varietal well-coloured wine that tastes of plums, berries, and spice.
- ■ **Light red** – Beaujolais Nouveau, a fresh Merlot or even a young Pinot Noir.
- ■ **Rosé** – Light, refreshing. Usually easy-drinking, undemanding sharing wine.
- ■ **Full white** – Shut your eyes and try to guess the colour. Examples will often be oak aged and have a bold mouthfeel. Expect notes of vanilla, butterscotch and even coconut.
- ■ **Dry whites** – Expect fresh, fruity, zesty flavours. Examples include Pinot Grigio, Sauvignon Blanc and Verdicchio at their very best.
- ■ **Sweet whites** – A German Riesling is a perfect example, however some might find a Gewürztraminer or a Muscat Blanc more extreme. If you have a sweet tooth, seek them out.
- ■ **Dessert wines** – Get out your smallest glasses for these, your biggest goblets just won't do. The sweetness of a Madeira or a noble rot wine such as Sauternes is to be enjoyed in the smallest of quantities.

Sparkling wines

A glass of bubbly? There is something about sparkling wine that explodes with style and sophistication. A glass of bubbly is the drink of choice for celebrants, rappers and for F1 racers who really should know better than to spray vintage wines over each other. Champagne has to be the best known, but there are other bubbling drinks which are equally good.

England is regarded as the home of the creation and proliferation of modern sparklers, probably around the middle of the 17th century. And it was technology – probably used by brewers – that made it happen. A sparkling wine, because of the pressure it creates, ideally needs a strong glass bottle and a cork stopper. The equipment to do this was available in England.

At the time, some writings seemed to suggest that bubbles in wine were a fault – before it became a drink of sophistication.

The Restoration dramatist Sir George Etherege is often credited for being the first to mention sparkling Champagne wines, in his comedy of manners *The Man of Mode* (1676).

Within just a few years, Champagne wines were all the rage in England, with the French following close behind in the 1700s.

It is likely that wine imported from France in barrels, which still contained living yeast, was bottled in England. And at some time before the end of the century the bottling technology had crossed the Channel to France.

So how do the bubbles get into sparkling wines? There are three basic ways: a second fermentation of a wine in a bottle, a second fermentation in a big tank or barrel, or by the addition of the fizz, which is carbon dioxide, artificially.

A secondary fermentation is a part of the fermentation process. Yeast converts sugar into alcohol, creating carbon

◀ **Champagne is regarded by some as the most sophisticated of sparkling wines.** (Cath Harries)

▶ **Sparkling wine is made in many parts of France. Cremant comes from Bordeaux.** (Cath Harries)

dioxide on the way. If yeast remains in contact with a wine which still has a little sugar in it, then fermentation can begin again.

To call a drink Champagne, it has to be made in the most northern winegrowing area of France. All Champagne is sparkling, but not all sparkling wines come from Champagne. The wine isn't made from a single grape variety, it is a blend. Three varieties are often used: Chardonnay, Pinot Noir and Pinot Meunier are the grapes of choice. It seems weird that Champagne, a white wine, is mainly made from black grapes.

Traditionally the grapes are handpicked and only the best will be harvested. The grapes are pressed as soon as possible after harvesting, and to this day most villages in the region have their own press.

Being French of course there are lots of local rules. Only certain grape varieties can be used if the maker wants the appellation accreditation, these being Chardonnay, Pinot Noir, Pinot Meunier, Pinot Blanc, Pinot Gris, Arbane and Petit Meslier.

There are restrictions on the methods of pruning: only the Royat, Chablis, Guyot and Vallée de la Marne systems can be used.

A limit is also placed on the weight of grapes which can be picked from a certain area. The aim is to optimise fruit quality through high-density (8,000 plants per hectare), low-yield vineyards. And once the pressing begins only a certain amount of juice can be taken from the fruit: yields are currently set at 102 litres of must per 160kg of grapes.

In addition to secondary fermentation, Champagne has to undergo a minimum period of maturation on lees – 15 months for non-vintage Champagne and three years for vintage.

So how is it made? A wine will be made from each of the component grape varieties. These individual wines will be allowed to mature to develop some of their flavours. The blending (assemblage) of the wines together has to begin; this involves lots of tasting and some chemical analysis of the wines. The skill of the blender is to carefully construct the blend from different vintages, pressings, grapes and villages.

Most Champagnes are not vintage and are instead cuvées. This means that the winemaker blends grapes from different years in order to maintain consistency in the taste of the drink. When the blend has been created, it will be bottled and primed with a little bit of wine, sugar and yeast – known in French as *liqueur de tirage*. A temporary seal is now put on the bottle and the bottles will now be laid out horizontally in the Champagne house's capacious cellar.

▶ **English sparkling wine is now among the best in the world.**
(Cath Harries)

▲ **The best sparkling wines are slowly moved from a horizontal position to vertical so yeast collects in the neck.** (Quartz Reef Wines)

SECONDARY FERMENTATION IN THE BOTTLE

A secondary fermentation will now begin in the bottle creating a little bit of alcohol, carbon dioxide and dead yeast cells. The carbon dioxide, having nowhere else to go, slowly dissolves into the wine. The dead yeast cells collect on the side of the bottle. The wine is then left in the bottle for a minimum of 15 months. Time is important to Champagne.

Next the sediment comprising the dead yeast cells has to be removed. The first stage of this is to move the bottle so that the sediment collects in the bottle's neck – a process known as *remuage*. Once this is done the sediment is removed, known as *degorgement*.

Remuage involves altering the position of the bottle from its horizontal position, which it has had for many months, to vertical with the top facing down. This process can be done by hand, in a rack which can hold many bottles. Each day the bottles will be carefully moved and inclined just a little more.

Today, there are machines which can alter the inclination of the bottle each day. Once the bottles are vertical with the top facing down, the neck of the bottle is frozen in a solution of saltwater. The bottles are then put the right way up. If all has gone well the temporary top will still be in place and the sediment will be hard up against the top, held in place by a plug of ice.

The temporary top is now removed and the pressure inside the bottle ejects the sediment and ice. The wine bottle will then be topped up with a little sugar and water and, moving quickly, the final cork will be firmly put in place and the top wired.

Sparkling wines from other regions of France include Vins Mousseux, Blanquette, Cremante and Frizzante. However, sparkling wines are made around the world from America to Korea and New Zealand. New World sparkling-wine makers have been quick to modernise production of the drink, saying they have speeded up the process and made it more economical without compromising on quality.

In Europe, Cava from Spain, Sekt from Germany and Austria, Asti and Prosecco in Italy are made using similar techniques.

SECONDARY FERMENTATION IN A TANK

Probably most sparkling wine drunk in the world undertakes its secondary fermentation in a large sealed tank, rather than a bottle. The wine is poured in, together with sugar and yeast, and the tank is sealed – a process known as *cuve close*. Once the secondary fermentation is finished the wine will be filtered and bottled.

CARBONATION

A third method of getting the bubbles into wine is by carbonation, but the carbon dioxide created during a secondary fermentation is not used. It is a cheap and cheerful way of creating bubbles. Carbon dioxide will be injected into the wine, but what goes in quickly, dissipates quickly once the bottle has been opened. The fizz quickly turns flat as the big bubbles burst.

Getting sweet on sherry

Sherry – does anyone drink it any more? Well, yes they do.

People should 'addict themselves to sack' said Falstaff in Shakespeare's play *King Henry the Fourth*.

Sack, or sherry as we now call it, is a drink with a long, proud heritage, Spanish in origin. Shakespeare goes on to say that it 'warms the liver and makes people loquacious and witty'. Well they do say a little alcohol encourages the art of conversation.

Sherry is a fortified wine, which means it is a mixture of a fully fermented wine, which is today produced almost exclusively from the Palomino Fino grape, and a spirit distilled from wine.

It takes its name from the town of Jerez, in the south of Spain, which once used to be the Moorish town of Sherish.

From early days it was a popular drink in England – and by the 1850s, records show, 40% of wine imported was sherry.

There are two styles of sherry – fino and oloroso – and a number of variations.

The difference between the two is a wild yeast, known as flor, which grows on the surface of wines in the fino family while they are in a barrel. The layer of yeast stops air getting to the wine and inhibits oxidation. This results in fresh and vivacious wines, with reduced acidity and increased acetaldehyde.

Sherries which do not develop flor belong to the oloroso family, which mature on contact with the air. This results in an oxidised wine with darker, richer and bolder inclinations.

Be it fino or oloroso, the wine starts off with the same must, which makes a wine known as mosta.

All sherry is fermented dry; sweetness if needed will be added later. At some stage the sherrymaker will decide the fate of each batch. To flor or not to flor? That is the question.

Traditionally, the base wine for sherry is fermented warmer than is usual for white wines, between 25° and 30°C. The mosta will be then fortified with an equal mixture of a strong spirit and an older wine.

Finos are fortified to 15.5% ABV; the flor can cope with alcohol of this strength, indeed it should thrive. Oloroso is fortified to 18% ABV, too strong for the flor yeast to prosper.

Next, the fortified wines have to be aged for at least two years, frequently longer, which helps to enhance the characteristics of the wine.

In the early days, sherry was no doubt aged in earthenware amphorae and jars. However, by the Middle Ages, most was already aged in wood, which was easier to transport. Today, wood is the material of choice for the biological ageing of sherry, using a system known as a solera.

It has probably taken a long time to evolve the system of linked wooden casks and lots of different woods have been used too, including chestnut, Spanish oak and American oak.

A solera is a series of linked barrels, which mixes wines of different ages and stages of maturation together. Traditionally, with a small sherrymaker, the solera comprises three rows of linked barrels. Each row contains blends of different ages, the youngest being at the top. With large sherrymakers, the layers of the solera are less likely to be stacked, instead the different 'levels' could be in different warehouses.

As some of the older wine is taken out of the solera to be bottled, newer wine mixes in with the remaining older wine. This newer wine is in turn replaced by even newer wine. It is introduced gently, so as not to disturb the flor. The barrels are never filled to the top, as space is left for the flor to develop.

When sold, a sherry must be at least three years old, but because of the solera system, some of it could be much older. The blending of wines of different vintages results in consistency and continuity. It is a continuous process of blending ageing wines, which take on their own unique character.

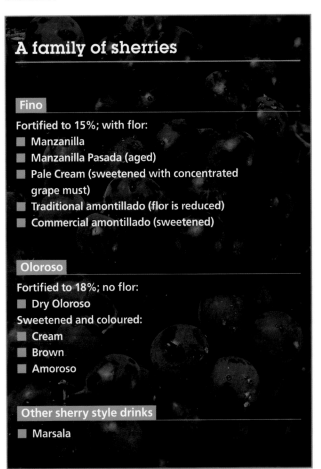

A family of sherries

Fino

Fortified to 15%; with flor:
- Manzanilla
- Manzanilla Pasada (aged)
- Pale Cream (sweetened with concentrated grape must)
- Traditional amontillado (flor is reduced)
- Commercial amontillado (sweetened)

Oloroso

Fortified to 18%; no flor:
- Dry Oloroso

Sweetened and coloured:
- Cream
- Brown
- Amoroso

Other sherry style drinks
- Marsala

(Cath Harries)

Any port in a storm?

Born in Portugal, port is a very British drink. Another fortified wine, it's made differently from sherry.

The process starts as with all other wines, with grapes. Traditionally, these are grown on the slopes of the Douro Valley. Dry and arid in the summer, even the stones seem to shiver in the winter, it can get so cold.

Here grapes are grown in small vineyards. Many grapes have names, however, some are unknown varieties. But they can all be used to make port.

Sweetness is an important characteristic of a port – this is achieved by fermenting the must to a strength between six and nine per cent alcohol. The immature wine will then be mixed with a spirit made from wine (brandy) which has a strength of 77% ABV, in a ratio of four parts wine to one part spirit.

The strength of the spirit will kill the yeast, leaving much of the residual sugar in the wine unfermented.

In the early days of making port, the process would have been similar to sherry. The spirit was added to a fully fermented dry wine. However, in 1820, a new method for adding the spirit started to be used, when the spirit was added before fermentation had finished, creating a sweeter blend. Port as we know it today was developing.

It was constant warring between Britain and France which first saw the appearance of a drink called port, during the second half of the 17th century. The British turned their attention to wines from Iberia in preference to wines from Bordeaux, which in 1678 were banned from importation into the British Isles for eight years.

At first there was a resistance to these wines from Oporto; they were rough and raw – but there was no Burgundy! Then it was discovered that when left for many years in wooden barrels and even blended with other wines, the rough became smooth. The ugly duckling had turned into a beautiful swan – the smooth drink we know as port.

Port can be a child of a single year or a blend of several. Some is matured in large wooden vats, other ports are left to age in a bottle. Most of it will be left to mature in wooden barrels in the port lodges of Oporto.

MAIN PORT STYLES

- White – not all ports are red. White ports can be dry or sweet; they are usually aged in wood and bottled when two to three years old.
- Ruby – full bodied, and matured in wood, they will be at least three years old, some are six.
- Tawny – some are blends of young ruby and white ports. Other have been wood-matured for many years and then blended. There will be aromas of wood and dried fruits.

Spirited wine

To make brandy, one of the world's best known spirits, first you need to make wine. The art of distillation probably began more than 3,500 years ago, somewhere in China or Mesopotamia.

But it was not until about 500 AD that wine was first distilled to make a spirit. Dionysus, the son of the Greek god Zeus, was the subject of elaborate ceremonies where a distillate was set alight and the resultant flames would honour the god of wine.

Moving on a thousand years or so to northern Italy, the practice of distillation was becoming more commonplace. And the concentrated, intense liquid which resulted was thought to have magical qualities and was called eau de vie, the water of life.

To make a spirit from wine, first the wine needs to be boiled. Alcohol boils at 78.5°C and water at 100°C. Once the temperature reaches 78.5° the alcohol start to boil off in the form of vapour, leaving the water behind. The distiller collects the alcohol vapour, cools it and has a stronger, concentrated liquid we call spirit.

Brandy is widely produced around the world, but the two best known brandies are Cognac and Armagnac, which come from different regions in France. Eau de vie is first mentioned in France in 1549, but it was 100 years or so before it became popular and was recognised as a drink rather than a medicinal potion, used to cure toothache, fever and other ailments.

To be called Cognac, the spirit has to be made in the French departments of Charente or Charente-Maritime. A wine is made to somewhere between 8% and 10% alcohol. It is distilled in a pot still two or three times, getting stronger each time. The clear distillate will be put into wooden barrels (usually made of oak) and left for at least two years.

As the alcohol ages, it mellows and takes on the flavour and colour of the wood. Eventually the liquid will be blended with other casks of brandy, and water will be added to reduce the alcohol to 40% prior to bottling.

Armagnac also comes from the south-west of France. Historically the drink claims to be older than Cognac, with some saying the Moors made it in the 12th century. Armagnac is usually distilled just once.

Like Cognac, Armagnac is stored in oak barrels, but need only be stored for one year before it can be drunk.

From Italy comes grappa, a fiery fresh spirit which is made from *marc*, the pulp and other debris which results from grapes being squashed to make wine. It is often drunk unaged.

In South America, Chile and Peru have a long history of making a wine-based spirit called Pisco.

The biggest selling brandy in the world, Presidente, is produced in Mexico where locals like to drink it mixed with cola.

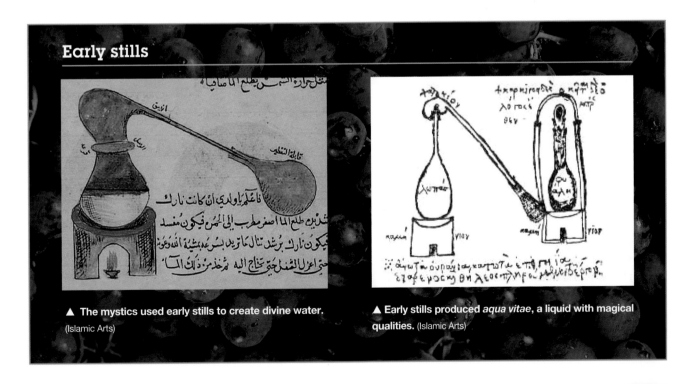

Early stills

▲ The mystics used early stills to create divine water.
(Islamic Arts)

▲ Early stills produced *aqua vitae*, a liquid with magical qualities. (Islamic Arts)

CHAPTER 4
WINE APPRECIATION

(Bordeaux Wine School)

Wine appreciation – don't bottle wine up – drink it

So you want to drink like a professional? Why, they usually spit their wine out.

And that's not because the wine is off. Professional tasters often have to sample scores of wines in a day, and they have to be cautious about how much alcohol they consume.

And sometimes, when tasting, professionals will do it blind. They sample wine in a darkened room from an opaque glass. They don't know the colour of the wine or anything about the vintage. You should try it sometime and discover how difficult it is to decide the colour of a wine with no clues other than the nose and taste of the wine.

We amateurs have it so much easier – we have our senses of sight, smell and taste, and it is likely we can see the bottle from which the wine is being poured.

However, with just a little bit of knowledge the joyful sipping of a glass of wine can become even more pleasing. Simple analysis of wines is not meant to be pretentious, instead it adds enjoyment to drinking a glass of wine.

The best way to enjoy a wine is to be in good company. Wine has fuelled many a good conversation, and most wine is not meant to be bottled up – it's meant to be drunk.

SIGHT

We drink with our eyes, our visual sense whets the appetite and sets the taste buds anticipating.

What is the colour of the wine? Is it clear? If it is cloudy this could indicate a fault. Unpretentiously we might say wine is red, white or sometimes rosé. This unassuming simplicity ignores the range of colours embraced by the descriptors red and white. The colour of a wine is a window into its inner soul and can give an indication of the style, age, taste and complexity of the wine.

An experienced taster will also see if the wine has 'legs' – these are traces of the wine which can be seen on the side of the glass after it has been swirled. Legs usually indicate that the wine is strong.

Whether the wine is red or white, each colour has many shades and experienced tasters will start to analyse the different hues by placing the glass in front of a white sheet of paper.

Red wine colours

The colour and opacity of a wine are the first steps in unlocking the mysteries of what is contained in the glass. What colour red is the wine? Is it light or dark? Is it crystal clear or dark and seemingly impervious to light? The colours can range from pink through brick to deep purple.

Light bodied

Lighter bodied reds are likely to be lower in tannins than their fuller red cousins. The colour ranges from magenta, a vibrant violet-red or purplish red colour through to the fuller, deeper garnet. A typical grape would be a fresh-tasting, easy-drinking

Pinot Noir. Another lower tannin grape is the Gamay, which underpins many a fine bottle of Beaujolais. These are easy-sipping and drinking wines, ones that will make you feel like having a second glass.

Medium bodied

Darker than its lighter cousins – expect an easy-drinking balanced duet of acidity and some tannins. Wines in this family could have been made with Zinfandel or Merlot grapes, firm favourites in California. Expect to see red berry and even some red cherry colours. Likely to be stronger than light bodied wines. The softer characteristics of these wines make them more suitable for drinking young.

Full bodied

Dark, with hues of purple, they are often opaque. Deep blues can be perceived – some are the colour of blackberries, dark plums or damsons. Expect a full mouthfeel as these wines are full of tannins. Fully attenuated, such wines are often strong in alcohol and may well have been matured in oak casks. They are made from the heavyweights of the grape world including Malbec, Syrah and Cabernet Sauvignon. On some a blueish rim may be perceived, which could indicate a lower acidity.

(Murdoch James Estate)

Older reds

If the wine in the glass is a lacklustre red or even a dull brown it could indicate that it is older and possibly past its prime. Expect to see some dull orange or transparent reds. Anticipate some oxidation and hints of spice.

Rosé

Expect to see pale red, pink and even poached salmon colours. In the best rosés the grapes will have been treated delicately and only lightly crushed. The grape skins will have been separated from the juice early in the production process. A rosé can be made from any red grape, but common varieties include Grenache, Sangiovese, Syrah and even Pinot Noir.

White wine colours

White wines have many shades and nuances, from a clear pale yellow to a golden, honey-tinged hue. Most are drunk while young and vivacious and are often best appreciated ice cold. In some white crystals known as tartrates can be seen; they don't affect the taste and are formed if the wine has been stored in cold conditions.

Lighter bodied

Expect to see clear pale citrus yellow hues, some with a green apple tinge. These wines are young and sprightly with the exuberance of a teenager. Typical grapes include Pinot Grigio and Muscadet. Expect some acidity.

Medium bodied

Probably the most popular wine style colour in the world. Pale yellow sun-kissed golds abound. Grapes can include Sauvignon Blanc, Chardonnay and Chenin Blanc. Expect easy-drinking wines.

Full bodied

Dark yellow, pine and oak colours. Low in acidity – expect to taste some oak and vanilla notes. Perhaps there will be some butter and creaminess. Some wines will have been aged in oak; grapes include the seemingly ubiquitous Chardonnay, Viognier and its often blending companion Marsanne.

Old white

There are not many white wines which get a chance to age. And those that reach a venerable age will have often have lost their sheen and look dull to the eye. Depending on how the wine has been stored it will often have taken on some orange notes as the liquid reacts to daylight.

TOUCH

What temperature is the wine in the glass? Each wine has an optimal serving temperature. For whites this is probably between 6° and 13°C. Too cold and undesirable characteristics can be hidden away. Crisp, acidic, citrus-flavoured wines should be served at the lower temperature. More robust whites prefer a warmer temperature.

Red wines benefit from being served a little warmer, from 11° to 18°C. Fruity reds do best at the lower end of the temperature range. Fuller reds embrace warmer temperatures.

As a general rule a cool crisp Sauvignon Blanc needs to be served cooler or the taste will be killed and its piquant delicacy muted. Big red Burgundies can show off their depth of flavour when warmer.

Rosés are normally served chilled.

The glass temperature is important. Too warm, if it is straight out of a dishwasher, will result in a disappointing experience.

SMELL

Now the nose has it. Given how sensitive our noses are, we really do not look after them. They can detect and discriminate between a myriad of aromas – there are more than 1,000. The nose picks up so many tastes that our tongue cannot detect. If the wine is a light white, can you detect some flowery or even citrus notes? Or are there hints of loganberry or blackcurrant? For just a moment resist taking a sip and let the aromas swirl and your nose do its work.

The French writer Marcel Proust (1871–1922), in his novel *À la recherche du temps perdu* (In search of lost time), describes a character vividly recalling long-forgotten memories from his childhood after smelling a tea-soaked madeleine biscuit. Now think wine. What recollections does the nose evoke?

TASTE

The time has come to take a sip and let it work its way around your mouth. As we are amateurs, we can swallow some. What can be detected – salt, sweet, bitter, sour, umami? Let the whole of the tongue do its work – a Muscat might give some blackberry flavours; other wines bring tropical fruit flavour to the glass. Does it taste young or old, immature or fulsome, fresh or musty?

Is the wine sweet or not? If it has a drying effect on the tongue this could be due to tannins. Does it have body? And finally, what is the alcohol content – is it low or high? A warmer taste at the back of your mouth probably indicates a stronger wine.

FINISHING OFF

Now as we are amateurs, we have a choice, either spit or swallow. Most of us like to swallow and experience the full effect of the wine. Is it warming? This could indicate it is stronger in alcohol. Does the sweetness linger?

What other flavours can you detect – perhaps there are different fruits or notes of vanilla or other spices? Is the finish short, medium or long? And most importantly, would you have another sip?

(Cath Harries)

Tasting like a professional

Berry Bros & Rudd manager Francis Huick describes how to taste like a professional and enjoy it.

▲ So to have a good bottle of wine the glassware is important – you don't need anything too flashy – you need a stem, so you take the glass by its feet. If you hold the ball, you'll warm the wine.

▲ The glass shape is important – a water glass is not appropriate – what you need to do is aerate the wine – this helps some of the flavours come out of the glass. It helps to release the more non-volatile aromas.

▲ Some people say you need a specific glass – but the most important thing is to have a glass you are comfortable with. I always like to smell the glass – can you smell chemicals from the water it was washed in, or dust?

▲ Never wash a glass in a dishwasher, just use running water. And rinse it with white or red wine vinegar and crystal salt to remove marks. Use a soft cloth to dry. And never put a glass upside down on a table – it can take on the smell of wax or polish. In some restaurants they'll hold a glass over boiling water to give it a final clean and make it crystal clear.

▲ Next we have to take the cork out. I always cut the foil below the rim. I do this because here might be some mould and this could fall into the wine. Wipe the top of the bottle to clean it.

▲ Take the corkscrew – the screw must not be too long – don't go through the cork, you can push sediment into the bottle. Some sommeliers use the cork itself to clean the top of the bottle.

▲ Now smell the cork. If the cork smells bad, it is unlikely the wine is good. You want to have a fresh, fruity smell. It is an indicator of what is in the bottle. It is a first step. The cork needs to be firm but subtle – it is the barrier to stop the wine ageing too quickly – a good cork allows a little air to get in but not too much.

▲ Now you serve a little bit and have a sniff. I trust my first impressions, if it's clean, it's good. Wine is not the same all the way through the bottle, so never shake a bottle. I always recommend to my customers to open the bottle early – and decant carefully.

▲ To pour – don't fill the glass, we are not filling a mug with tea – fill the glass up to one-third, that makes it easier to swirl. To pour, basically count in seconds one, two, three, four, five, six, seven seconds.

(All photos Cath Harries)

▲ Now, take the first look at what you are going to drink – put a piece of white paper behind it so you can see the colour. Pinot Noir has a good transparency of colour – always a cheery raspberry red – always bright. The wine should look healthy – a young wine will be vivid, it becomes darker as it gets older. Has it a good transparency of colour, is it intense, is it bright? If it is turbid it might mean there has been some refermentation or it hasn't been filtered. It doesn't necessarily mean it is bad.

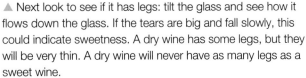 Next look to see if it has legs: tilt the glass and see how it flows down the glass. If the tears are big and fall slowly, this could indicate sweetness. A dry wine has some legs, but they will be very thin. A dry wine will never have as many legs as a sweet wine.

Next have another sniff – is it clean, is it pleasant – is it fruity, dark or red, floral fresh, is it earthy or animal? This is clean and elegant – red fruit and floral tones – raspberry and redcurrant – there is some acidity. Behind it there is some rose – there are some grassy notes.

▶ Now take a taste. Swirling brings out different intensities – it's like a piece of music with different notes at different times. This wine has been aged on its lees – there is some cherry, a bit of spice – a soft feel like a cloth – some silk, but these are my personal perceptions.

He spits it out and takes another taste. It's smoky too – it's complex, that doesn't mean it's difficult but there is a lot to it – and it changes the longer it has been opened. Predominantly fresh, at this stage you should taste the wine slowly.

This is characteristic of a Pinot Noir: it is gentle but has some power – easy to approach, it is a friendly wine on the palate, it is what you had in the aroma. Fine tannins. Here the tannins are good, no aggressivity – some wine can be harsh.

It has a good freshness, finish is spicy – it is a good wine. This is a friendly wine to help discussion – if you want to be left alone to meditate you need something more austere. Emotions are important – a wine for today might not be the wine for tomorrow.

(Cath Harries)

Caring for and serving wine

Most of us just keep the white wine in a fridge or put bottles of red on a shelf in the kitchen until we're ready to drink it.

Most of the time we probably get away with it. Yet, with a little more thought about care and storage the enjoyment of the wine could be enhanced.

Too often the temperature of the wine is overlooked. If stored at too warm a temperature (above 20°C), wine can start to age and lose its flavour. If too cool, flavour and aroma will be lost.

The ideal range of temperature for storing red wine is 10° to 16°C. White wines can be stored at a lower temperature – around 6°C. (Though of course most fridges are set to 4°C.) By the oven or near a radiator during winter is likely to be too hot, a garage is likely to be too cold.

When most wine bottles were sealed with a cork, the advice was to store it on its side, so the cork wouldn't dry out. Once dry, a cork cracks and can let air into the bottle and oxidise the wine. But in an era of screw caps, standing wine bottles up is fine.

Also, it is best to keep bottles out of sunlight, as ultraviolet light can break down wine.

Cheap and cheerful bottles from a supermarket or off licence are best drunk soon after purchase. Laying wines down for storage of longer than a few weeks isn't difficult, but it is best to get it right for the wine to keep well.

The storage temperature is not necessarily the same as serving temperature. Wine should be served at a temperature that best reveals its characteristics and aromas.

The optimal serving temperature differs for various wines, depending on their grape variety and their region. If you have just bought a bottle of rich, intense Bordeaux or a forceful Californian Cabernet Sauvignon then the profound flavours will be enhanced if the wine is a little below room temperature – say about 18°C. Big reds often need some time to reach the best serving temperature. A fresh, fruity Beaujolais on the other hand could be at its best between 10° and 12°C, and a sparkling white wine will need more chilling.

Some wines benefit from aerating and decanting. This is achieved by pouring the wine into a decanter. Aerating a wine can soften the tannins in a young, tannin-rich Bordeaux. The callow wine becomes softer and smaller. Some say a young wine should be aerated, which brings air into contact with the wine, for six hours to allow the flavours to develop.

An old, mature wine shouldn't be aerated for so long. If left for too long the fragile aromas, part of the sensual experience of an older wine, will be lost.

A wine which has a sediment is often best poured into a decanter before serving. With careful pouring the sediment will remain in the bottle, the best place for it.

And when drinking outside on a warm summer's day beware, the contents of a bottle will often heat up quite quickly. This can spoil the fragile bouquet of a delicate white. An ice bucket filled with cold water and ice is just perfect.

Wine and food – a perfect marriage

Wine and food pairing? Yes, we do it all the time.

But is there any art or science to it, or is it just eating a little of what you fancy with a glass or two of your favourite tipple?

Some wine experts will tell you there is a food for every wine. Well, yes there might be.

But the old adage of saying that red wines should only be eaten with red meats, or reach for a bottle of white when eating chicken or a piece of fish, is not that helpful.

Thank goodness that we live in an age when most people think such stringent, rigid rules are nothing but vinous snobbery. There are no rules, only hints as to what can work.

If you like the match, then the match is right. The key to successful matching is to know the wine you want to pair, and the dish you are going to eat it with – understand their characteristics and flavours. Is the wine sweet or dry? Is it spicy or fruity? Then what is the flavour profile of the food – is it light and delicate, would it be easily overpowered by the fullness of some wines?

According to the Australian winemakers Jacob's Creek, if you are a snacker then Shiraz with spicy fruit plum flavours can harmonise with the strong aromatic herbs and salty cheese that make a Margherita pizza.

If you believe them, a glass of Riesling is perfect to quaff with a sausage roll. Often Rieslings will have green apple, acidic and butter flavours, and these will augment the sweetness of pork sausage meat and the fat in the pastry.

Those who like rich, sweetish chocolate should reach for the screw cap and open a bottle of soft fruit-flavoured Merlot. But beware, not all chocolate is sweet and a bitter chocolate might be better off with a different pairing. And while watching a favourite movie and munching a bowl of salted popcorn, you should reach for a glass of Sauvignon Blanc.

If having more than one wine with a meal, the order in which they are drunk can influence appreciation. Generally it is best to drink dry before sweet. A dry aperitif will often prepare the palate for food. Sweeter wines and those low in acidity tend to numb our taste buds, so these are often better towards the end of a meal. For this reason sparkling wines are often best drunk before a still wine. A dry-ish glass of bubbles can be palate-cleansing.

When considering a pairing you want both the food and wine to shine – either separately or together. If the flavours are fighting against each other then it is probably not a good match.

It is also best to start off with wines lower in alcohol. The greater fullness and body of a stronger wine will overwhelm the delicate nature of a lower alcohol wine, which can seem feeble and unattractive if drunk second.

When building a drinks list, youth should often go before age. Younger wines, as a very general rule, are more vivacious and ephemeral than their elders. Complexity, richness and elegance are attributes which come with age.

Wine is a sublime ingredient in food. And there are many classic recipes which include wine – such as coq au vin, or as most people call it, chicken casserole. It can be cooked with a white or a red wine and one that is dry or sweet. Whichever is chosen, the same style of wine is best drunk with the meal.

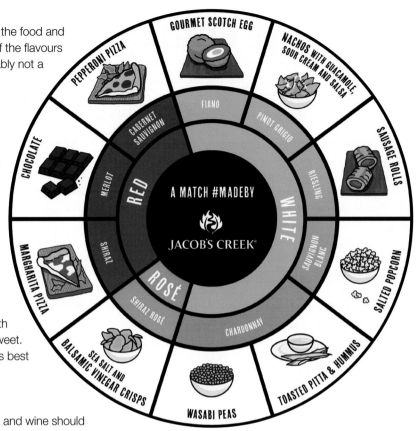

(Jacob's Creek)

PAIRING HINTS

Pair shared flavours and characters. The food and wine should complement and not overpower each other. Delicate dishes are best with delicate wines. Robust, sweet and spicy burgers need a rich full-bodied wine.

Hot, spicy dishes are often best with wines that are lower in tannins and alcohol. Look for something which has some sweetness.

Contrasting foods and wines can also be good partners, but they are harder to achieve. A heavy chicken dish which is rich in cream can be counterbalanced by a dry, white, crisp wine.

Be aware of bitterness in a dish, it is unlikely to partner well with a high tannin wine. Such wines go well with fatty food and those with salt and umami.

Usually, the wine should be sweeter than the food. If it's the other way around the sweetness of the food can bring out bitterness in the wine.

Acidity is like sweetness – you want it to be higher in the wine than in the dish. An acidic vinaigrette can make some wines seem flabby and dull.

Finally, remember there are no hard and fast rules, only personal preferences!

GRAPE PAIRINGS

Chardonnay

Pasta in a light, cream sauce. The buttery flavours in both can be complementary. Chicken, pork and salads will pair well. However, a Chardonnay might contrast with a rich crab dish.

Gewürztraminer

A favourite with Chinese, Indian or Thai food. Also works well with sweet desserts.

Pinot Noir

A classic pairing with rich game dishes, such as pheasant, hare or venison.

Sauvignon Blanc

Fresh asparagus with a butter sauce. Chicken, fish and shellfish work well, even those with a squeeze of lemon. The wine has enough body to work with spicy dishes.

Semillon

A willing partner to many fish dishes, it can also cope with roast or barbecued chicken glazed in honey.

Syrah

Bold beef dishes and barbecued food.

Red Zinfandel

Rich red meat dishes.

White Zinfandel

It goes with just about anything cooked on a barbecue. Try it with rich creamy cheeses.

Cooking with wine

Adding wine to a dish can transport the ordinary into the sublime.

But as ever, a little knowledge goes a long way. Wine contains alcohol, acid, tannins and sugars, and some attribute of each of these will end up in the final dish. Though some cooking processes will dissipate alcohol and subtle flavours will often be lost.

Creative cooks will often add a splash of wine to many dishes, even if it's not in the recipe. But beware – if the dish already contains vinegar, or the juice of a lemon or lime, the addition of wine can overwhelm it.

And while the rule is neither hard nor fast, if you've prepared a dish with a wine – then when you come to eat it, pair it with a similar wine.

CHEESE FONDUE

One of the great delights of wine drinking is sharing a bottle with friends and family.

One of the world's greatest recipes using wine is cheese fondue. It is the perfect dish for sharing. A dish which has its origins in Switzerland, it is the perfect early evening meal for a group of people weary after a long walk.

Serves four

Ingredients

- 200g Gruyere cheese, grated
- 200g Emmentaler cheese, grated
- 2 or 3 tablespoons white flour or cornflour
- 1 garlic clove, halved
- 250 ml dry white wine – such as a Sauvignon Blanc
- 1 teaspoon fresh lemon juice
- 1 dash kirsch, a Swiss or German fruit brandy (optional)
- Fresh ground pepper, to taste
- 1 pinch nutmeg
- Crusty bread, cut into large cubes, or a baguette sliced
- Green salad

Equipment

- Fondue pot, though a steel or enamel-lined cast iron saucepan can be used.

Method

1 In a bowl mix the grated cheeses together and toss with the flour.
2 Rub the inside of the fondue pot with the garlic halves.
3 Add the wine and heat over medium heat until hot, but not boiling.
4 Stir in lemon juice and a dash of kirsch (optional).
5 Add a handful of cheese at a time to the wine mixture, stirring constantly. When it is melted add another handful, and keep melting and stirring until all the cheese is in the pot and melted.
6 The sauce should be light and creamy and bubbling gently.
7 Season with pepper and nutmeg.
8 Remove the pot from the heat and place over a fondue heater on the table.
9 Ideally, the cheese should continue to bubble very gently.
10 Everyone at the table can take turns dipping in hunks of bread.
11 Eat with a green salad.

(Tim Hampson)

COQ AU VIN

For a hungry four

Wine adds class to what might otherwise be a dull chicken casserole. And even before you serve the dish, the aromas from the kitchen will impress your guests. There are so many variations on this dish, that there is no definitive recipe. Some prefer to cook it slower for a longer time. It's up to you, but after trial and probably no errors, you will find what works for you, which can become a firm family favourite.

Traditionally as the name implies it was made with a male bird, however, either gender will do.

Ingredients

For the casserole

- 1.5kg chicken pieces, or a whole jointed chicken. Some people like to remove the skin, but you will also be losing some intense fatty flavours.
- 200g diced bacon or lardons, smoked or unsmoked, whichever is your preference.
- Two large onions, peeled and diced.
- One good glug or three tablespoons of olive oil.
- Good, large pat of butter. Other spreads can be used.
- One sprig of rosemary, more if you like it.
- Couple of sprigs of thyme.
- A healthy pinch of chilli flakes, a small teaspoonful (optional).
- A bay leaf.
- 600ml dry white/red wine, the rest of the bottle is for the chef.
- 400g small mushrooms – chestnut is good, but any will do.
- Three or four healthy garlic cloves, chopped.
- Good handful of chopped parsley.
- Tablespoon of white flour or cornflour, mixed into a good pat of butter or spread.

Method

1. Heat the oven up to 200°C, 180°C if it's a fan oven. Or the dish can be cooked on top of the stove on a low to medium heat.
2. Heat the oil and butter in a casserole dish or a frying pan. When hot, brown the chicken pieces on all sides. Don't cram the chicken when frying – you might have to fry it in batches.
3. Remove the chicken, and fry the bacon lardons until browned.
4. Remove the lardons, add the onion and garlic, heat for five minutes until soft.
5. Remove the onions and garlic.
6. Put the chicken, bacon, onion and garlic into the casserole dish.
7. Pour over the wine and add the rosemary, thyme and chilli or bay leaf.
8. Put lid on the casserole dish and put in the oven, or on a simmering heat on top of the stove.
9. After about 45 minutes add the mushrooms and stir.
10. Cook the casserole for another 15 minutes.
11. Using a slotted spoon remove the chicken and other ingredients from the casserole, and put into a serving dish. Discard the rosemary, thyme and bay leaf.
12. On top of the stove, bring the liquid to a fast boil for about five minutes. Lower the heat slightly and add the flour and butter/spread mix.
13. Keep stirring the sauce until it has thickened.
14. Pour the sauce over the cooked chicken and other ingredients.
15. Sprinkle with the chopped parsley and serve.

(Shutterstock)

BOEUF BOURGUIGNON

For four to six people

A retro French classic, which was once a staple of many wine bars, which is making a comeback. And with good reason, it's rich comfort food.

Ingredients

- 1kg of braising steak, cut into 5cm cubes.
- 200g diced bacon or lardons, smoked or unsmoked, whichever is your preference.
- Two or three garlic cloves, chopped.
- Two large onions, peeled and diced.
- Couple of sprigs of thyme.
- One bay leaf.
- One heaped tablespoon of white flour.
- 500ml of red Burgundy.
- 200g mushrooms – chestnut is good, but any will do.
- Three tablespoons of olive oil.
- Salt and pepper to taste.

Method

1 Heat the oven up to 140°C.
2 Heat two tablespoons of oil in a large casserole, and in batches brown the cubes of beef on all sides.
3 Remove the beef, add the bacon/lardons and fry until just browned.
4 Remove the lardons, add the onion and fry gently to add some brown colour, but do not burn.
5 Now put the browned beef and lardons, onion and garlic back into the casserole dish, sprinkle the flour over and stir well, to soak up all the juices.
6 Slowly pour in the wine and continue stirring.
7 Season with salt and pepper and add the thyme and bayleaf.
8 Put the lid on the casserole and cook for two hours in the oven.
9 After two hours add the sliced mushrooms and cook for a further hour.
10 Serve with mashed potato.

CHICKEN, PEA AND WHITE WINE RISOTTO

Suitable for four people

So you didn't use all the chicken that you roasted at the weekend? Here's a way of making a quick and easy risotto.

Ingredients

- Two tablespoons olive oil.
- One good sized onion, peeled and grated.
- Two cloves of garlic, crushed.
- 250g risotto rice.
- 100ml dry white wine.
- One litre chicken stock, made with a stock cube is fine.
- 250 to 300g cooked chicken – remove the skin and dice.
- 200g frozen peas.
- 75g Parmesan cheese, grated.
- 25g butter.
- For seasoning, freshly ground black pepper.

Method

1 In a large saucepan heat the oil on a medium heat. It should be hot, but not smoking.
2 Add the onion and garlic and gently fry for three minutes or so, stirring several times, until softened and just beginning to colour.
3 Add the risotto rice to the pan and stir very well for 30 to 40 seconds, until the oil has coated all of the rice.
4 Pour in half of the wine and let it quickly come to the boil and bubble, for 30 to 40 seconds, then add the stock and bring back to the boil. Keep stirring. Lower the heat and simmer in an uncovered pan for 8 to 10 minutes, stirring all the time, until the rice is almost cooked.
5 Stir in the rest of the wine, the diced chicken and the frozen peas. Keep stirring for a further five minutes or until the rice is tender but with a slight bite.
6 Remove the pan from the heat, stir in the butter and cheese. Season with black pepper. Cover the pan with a lid and set aside for five minutes to let the flavours develop before serving.

(Shutterstock)

(Tim Hampson)

MUSSELS IN WINE

A quick sharing supper or lunch for fans of mussels

Cooking mussels couldn't be easier – within moments a dish worthy of a top class restaurant can be produced. And like many of the best recipes, it makes a great sharing dish.

Ingredients

- 1kg mussels, cleaned or uncleaned.
- A glug of olive oil.
- One small onion, chopped.
- Two garlic cloves, chopped.
- 100ml dry white wine.
- 100ml double cream or crème fraiche.
- Large handful of fresh parsley, chopped.
- Crusty bread, to serve.

Method

1 If needed, clean and debeard the mussels. Discard any open mussels which don't close when tapped.
2 Heat the olive oil in a heavy pan. Add the onion and garlic and gently cook until soft, but not brown.
3 Pour in the wine and bring to the boil for a minute.
4 Add the mussels to the pan. Add most of the chopped parsley, cover the pan with a lid and cook for about three or four minutes, giving the pan a shake from time to time. The mussels are ready when they've opened up.
5 Sprinkle in the remaining parsley, then spoon the mussels into a serving bowl, discarding any which are not open.
6 Add the cream or crème fraiche to the remaining liquor, warm through and stir.
7 Pour the liquid over the mussels and serve in bowls with lots of crusty bread.

BARBECUED SEA BASS

Ingredients

- Four cleaned and gutted sea bass – each about 300g.
- Three large oranges – sliced.

For the wine marinade
- 150 ml white wine.
- Zest of one lemon.
- Zest of one of the oranges.
- One onion, peeled and thinly sliced.
- One tablespoon of olive oil.

Method

1 Slash each fish two or three times down each side
2 Finely grate the zest of one of the oranges, add to the lemon zest. Mix with the olive oil and wine. Pour over the fish, and gently rub into the flesh and season. Marinate for about an hour in a fridge.
3 Cut the oranges into slices about 4–5cm thick. When the barbecue is hot place the oranges in four lines on to the grill, each about one fish length long. Char on one side, flip over and put the fish on top.
4 The slices of orange will stop the fish sticking to the grill.
5 Cook the fish for about six minutes on one side and then carefully flip over and cook for another six minutes, or until the fish is cooked and flaked.
6 Serve.

The slices of charred orange can make a tasty snack in their own right.

(Tim Hampson)

SPAGHETTI COOKED IN RED WINE

Boiling pasta in red wine might sound a little bizarre, but it makes a dish fit not just for vegetarians but for anyone who likes flavoursome food.

Ingredients

- 1,200ml water.
- 200ml dry red wine.
- 350g spaghetti.
- 200ml virgin olive oil.
- Four garlic cloves, sliced.
- A good pinch of crushed red pepper.
- Good handful of parsley, finely chopped.
- 120g pine nuts, toasted and coarsely chopped.
- 300g Parmesan cheese, grated.
- Salt and freshly ground black pepper.

Method

1. Pour the water and 120ml wine into a saucepan with a good shake of salt and bring to a boil.
2. Add the spaghetti and cook, stirring occasionally, until soft with a little bit of bite. Drain, reserving 100ml of the cooking liquid.
3. In a saucepan heat two tablespoons of the olive oil, add the garlic and red pepper and season with salt. Cook over a gentle heat for one minute.
4. Add the remaining 80ml of wine and the reserved cooking liquid and bring to a simmer.
5. Stir in the pasta and cook until the liquid nearly disappears, probably about two minutes. Add the parsley, pine nuts, 250g of the cheese and the remaining oil. Toss everything well together.
6. Season the pasta with salt and pepper and serve with sprinkles of cheese.

Wine and health

The belief that wine is part of a healthy lifestyle goes back to the beginning of modern times. The Greek physician Hippocrates considered wine to be a part of a healthy diet. He also advised that it should be used to clean wounds and as a medium into which other drugs could be put to make them palatable.

Modern medical science seems to agree that moderate consumption of wine can have some beneficial effects, especially as part of the so-called Mediterranean diet (little meat, plenty of fish, fruit and salads). But the key word is moderation!

As they say, a little of what you fancy will do you good, and I'm sure we'll all raise a glass to that.

(Tim Hampson)

SPARKLING WINE JELLY

Some regard sparkling wine as luxury in a glass. Well a glass of the bubbles can also make the perfect light dessert to enjoy at the end of a rich meal.

Ingredients

- 20g pack leaf gelatine.
- 750ml sparkling wine – Cava or Prosecco is perfect, and you can choose white or rosé.
- 75g caster sugar.
- 150g mixed berries, fresh or frozen.
- Six tablespoons of cold water.

Method

1 Soak seven sheets of gelatine in six tablespoons of cold water for 10 minutes.
2 Measure 150ml of the sparkling wine and put it into a pan with the caster sugar. Heat the liquid gently until the sugar dissolves.
3 Squeeze out the gelatine and add to the pan, stir until dissolved, then pour in the remaining sparkling wine.
4 Pour into six attractive wine or martini glasses and add an equal mixture of fruit to each glass. Chill for four hours or overnight to set.

(Shutterstock)

(Tim Hampson)

SYLLABUB

A sweet treat for six people

Ingredients

- 250g ripe strawberries, destalked and sliced. Raspberries or blackberries could also be used.
- Four tablespoons caster sugar.
- 50ml sweet white dessert wine or a light sweet red.
- 300ml double cream.
- 300ml fat-free natural yoghurt.
- A few sprigs of fresh mint, to serve.
- One packet of all-butter biscuits.

Method

1 Put the strawberries in a bowl, sprinkle over the sugar and pour over the wine. Put aside for a few minutes.
2 In a separate bowl, whip the cream until it forms some nice soft peaks. Carefully stir in the yoghurt.
3 Fold half of the cream and yoghurt mix into the strawberries. Gently mix well, you want the mixture to take on the red colour of the strawberries.
4 Now, carefully fold in the remaining cream and yoghurt and mix to create a ripple effect.
5 Put the mixture into six attractive glasses.
6 Decorate with mint leaves and the butter biscuits.

Investing in wine – a corking success?

The wine in your cellar could literally become a bottle bank if you have invested wisely. It used to be said that an English gentleman should buy six cases of claret and put them in his cellar for ten years, then drink three of them and sell the other three. And by doing so he'd have more than enough money to buy another six.

Jura Vin Jaune
1774
Jura
62cl

£72,553.80

Today, there are people who make a corking success by investing in wines. But you have to get it right otherwise you could be whining all the way to the bank, though the bonus is that at least you can drink your negative equity.

It's a big market – the fine wine investment market is currently valued at $4 billion. Most trading takes place in 'en primeur', also known as wine futures. It is the practice of buying wine before it's bottled and released on to the market. Wines can only be purchased by the unmixed case (12 bottles, 24 half bottles, 6 magnums) and are usually delivered two or three years after the vintage.

The Wine Investment Association: www.wineinvestmentassociation.org says fine wine can be a rewarding, safe and enjoyable investment when executed properly, but the market is unregulated, so let the buyer beware.

But get it right and the results can be eye-watering. The author Roald Dahl once wrote that his favourite wine was Romanée-Conti. Indeed in his book *My Uncle Oswald*, Dahl wrote of the wine, 'Sense for me this perfume! Breathe this bouquet! Taste it! Drink it! But never try to describe it! Impossible to give an account of such a delicacy with words!'

◀ **A collector's item? Hedonism Wines in Mayfair, London, stocks some of the world's most expensive wines.** (Cath Harries)

▼ **Wines from the idiosyncratic Californian winery Sine Qua Nan are much sought after by buyers at Hedonism.** (Cath Harries)

SQN
Black and Blue
1992
California
75cl

£5,468.70

▲ **Bottles of Roald Dahl's favourite wine are bought for huge prices by collectors.** (Cath Harries)

Praise indeed and when recently a case of six magnums of 1970 Romanée-Conti, Domaine de la Romanée Conti was put up to auction in San Francisco, it sold for more than £36,000. The wine came from the estate of San Franciscan surgeon Maurice Galante, an avid collector of wines who had kept them in his purpose-built cellar for many years.

There are three ways to invest in wine. You could find a wine fund, use a wine merchant, or buy and sell cases yourself.

A good place to start is the internet. There are plenty of websites aimed solely at buyers and sellers of wines. These sites allow people to buy and sell products at agreed prices and see photos and videos of the wine they are considering investing in. The best ones will have information on current prices, price changes and developments in the market.

One such site is the Liv-ex (www.liv-ex.com), operated by the London International Vintners Exchange. It's a marketplace for fine wine and is a good place to check out your hunches and follow the progress of some of the world's hottest fine wines.

Founded in 2000 by two former stockbrokers, James Miles and Justin Gibbs, it brings together a fragmented marketplace and makes fine wine trading more transparent, efficient and safer.

It provides its members with access to 30,000 price changes per day, including live bids and offers, transaction prices, merchant list prices and auction hammer prices.

Wine Owners (www.WineOwners.com) is another wine trading exchange platform.

Founded by Nick Martin, his experience as a wine collector and enthusiast was typical. He found it hard to keep an up-to-date record of his wines and to track his total aggregate outlay, whilst the process of valuation and evaluation was desperately time-consuming. He says you would need a few thousand pounds to start a wine investment portfolio and you do not have to spend it all at once.

One of the doyens of en primeur is the recently retired Robert Parker. Such is his effect on the Bordeaux market that the Wine Investment Fund uses his scores of each wine as one of three pillars, along with the brand value of an individual chateau and reputation of the vintage, by which it measures the relative value of one wine against another.

Parker's influence has been profound – for instance Smith Haut Lafitte 2009 traded for £600–700 per case until February 2012, when he upgraded his rating from 96–98+ to a perfect 100 points. Almost immediately the wine shot up in value by 150% on Liv-ex.

But what goes up can go down, and there are examples of wines which have been given Parker's perfect 100 but which over time have fallen in price.

And remember, always be warned: it doesn't matter how much knowledge you have or advice you take, investing in wine is not always rosy and market slumps could leave you with a bad hangover. But with a little research your wine punt could turn to a handsome profit.

TOP TIPS

Don't be a victim of wine fraud – Be warned, there are people out there who will try to pressurise you into rash investments. Take your time and don't be rushed. And beware of promises of fast returns – investing in wine is a medium- to long-term activity.

Choose a reputable wine merchant – Get to know the wine merchant and do some homework on the firm's reputation. A good wine merchant will not make claims of guaranteed returns on your investment.

Know exactly what you are buying – Find everything out about the wine, where and when it was made and check out how well other vintages from the vineyard are doing. What is its provenance, quality and condition?

Look after your investment – How you store and manage your investment is crucial to its future value. The wine can be kept at home but it is usually better to have it professionally stored.

Understand the small print – Make sure you are clear what commission, charges and additional taxes you will have to pay on your investments.

Know when to drink or sell your collection – Wine's value drops after its ideal maturity, which differs for each grape and is affected by the wine's region or vintage. A good Bordeaux might peak after 15 years; a premium Burgundy could be at its best in eight years. If you plan to sell your wine, you might obtain the best price one to three years before it peaks.

(Bonhams)

INVESTMENT CHECKLIST

◼ Does the buyer or seller have a good reputation? Do an internet search on them.

◼ How long have they been in business? Be cautious of companies which are newly set up.

◼ Where are they based?

◼ Are their prices competitive? Go compare.

◼ What is the provenance of the wine? Find out everything you can about the wine.

◼ How much are commission, storage or delivery charges? Hidden charges could soon dent potential profits.

◼ Will your wine be stored separately from the company's other wines? Is the wine clearly identified as yours?

◼ What documents will you get to provide proof of purchase? Check that all documents are in order.

◼ Is your wine insured? It's always best to check what will happen if a calamity occurs.

WINE AUCTIONEERS

Bid for Wine

www.bidforwine.co.uk

Bonhams

020 7447 7447
www.bonhams.com

Christies

020 7930 6074
www.christies.com

Corney & Barrow

020 7265 2410
www.corneyandbarrow.com

Sotheby's

020 7293 5000
www.sothebys.com

Sworders Fine Wine Auctioneers

012 7981 7778
www.sworder.co.uk

An ultra-rare bottle of Château Mouton Rothschild 1945 was sold to a private collector by auction house Bonhams for more than £10,000. The bottle sold for less than it could have, however, because of concerns that it might be oxidised; there is too much space between the wine and the bottom of the cork.

Had it been in better condition, the 70-year-old bottle could have sold for twice as much.

But despite its potential undrinkability, the bottle is of huge historical significance because of the 'V' printed on the label, which is said to celebrate the Allies' victory over Nazi Germany in World War 2.

Educations in intoxication

Once wine bars in the City of London were two a penny. They began as a fad of the 1970s, when new money, economically independent women, the introduction of credit cards and the then failure of pubs to appeal to anyone save middle-aged men, saw them prosper. However, fashions changed and many have now closed down.

Today, 'wine-centric' bars and restaurants have once again emerged as one of the latest trends – paying homage to great drinks, interesting food and good living. A good wine bar has much more than glasses, fine wine, company and conversation; it offers the opportunity to learn more about wine from the staff, the menu or even the name of the bar.

GORDON'S WINE BAR

Superb service, standards and sublime simplicity. A family owned bar, Gordon's has been serving great wine, good food and offering dark alcoves for heated conversations for more than a century.

For an old place, the crowd at Gordon's Wine Bar are surprisingly young. The small ground floor bar has old wooden walls covered in historical newspaper cuttings and memorabilia faded with age. If this was the extent of the bar,

it would still be a classic. However, there is something deeply entrancing about the bar's low ceilinged basement vaults, which have exposed brickwork and are illuminated by the candles flickering on the rickety tables.

And outside, Watergate Walk, there are plenty of tables and chairs for those who prefer their wine al fresco.

In 1975 Luis Gordon bought the wine bar, which coincidentally bore the name of an unrelated Gordon whose family had run the bar since 1890. His ambition was simple, to maintain the bar as the customers like it – which basically meant 'no change'. The décor has remained unchanged for years, there is no juke box or gaming machine, just good wine and simple food. Perfect.

The original Gordon family were among the last of London's free vintners. Such people had the right to sell wine in certain parts of London without a licence. The privilege goes back to

(Cath Harries)

▲ ▼ ▶ **The passage of time is marked by collections of old bottles, photographs and newspaper cuttings at Gordon's Wine Bar in London.** (Cath Harries)

1364, when Edward III is said to have created them in an effort to pay off his wine debts.

Old Gordon's it might be, but it is not stuck in the past; the wine list keeps pace with developments in the world of viticulture. Unsurprisingly there are classics from the great wine-producing regions of France, Italy and Spain, but there is more than a passing nod to New World wines from South America and Australia.

▲ Just like the old days, sherry is sold straight from the barrel.
(Cath Harries)

Behind the bars are casks of fortified wines from which staff draw glasses of port, sherry and Madeira. Before the development of glass bottles all wine would have been served in this way.

The food is wonderfully uncomplicated and includes homemade pies, mature cheeses and plates of olives. In the summertime, customers can spill out of the cellar's semi-darkness and enjoy the terrace outside in Watergate Walk. Here on warmer days the staff need no excuse to fire up the barbecue and start to flip burgers.

The bar is a London landmark and is reputed to be the oldest surviving wine bar in the country. The building is much older than the bar – the great diarist Samuel Pepys lived here in the 1680s. It then became a warehouse with access to the river, but this ended when the embankment was built in 1864.

Laurence Olivier and Vivien Leigh are said to have enjoyed the intimacy of the candle-lit alcoves, while sipping on glasses of wine. And Tennyson and Chesterton are among many of the literary luminaries who have lunched here. Rudyard Kipling lived in the building in the 1890s as a tenant and famously wrote the novel *The Light that Failed* in the parlour above the bar.

▶ Gordon's manager, Gerard Menan loves to talk wine.
(Cath Harries)

Gordon's knowledgeable manager, Gerard Menan, hails from the Loire Valley region of France. It's a region rightly famed for its wines.

When asked to choose six of his favourite wines it would have been easy for Gerard to choose his six solely from the Muscadets he grew up with, or the Sancerres and Pouilly Fumés. Instead his passion for seeking out great wines sees him travel the world without leaving his bar.

It would be impossible for Gerard not to include something from his beloved Loire. This 2013 Sauvignon Blanc from the Domaine Les Petits Faiteaux in the Touraine region is fulsome, dry and crisp with a marvellous mineral finish and swathes of fresh herb aromas. It is the perfect partner with goats' cheese, green salad and dry crusty bread. It's a wine for sharing and good conversation.

Spain makes some great wines, and it is renowned for its sherry. In Britain most people drink sherry as an aperitif, missing out on its possibilities to partner food. Gerard recommends a bone dry, nutty flavoured Manzanilla sherry from Barbadillo. Long aged and matured, it is full bodied and vibrant, which because of its dry salty note makes it a perfect partner with shellfish.

The vines of Chile's largest winemaker, Concha y Toro in the Central Valley, are protected from the worst of the elements by the rocky embrace of the Andes. This creates a micro-climate ideal for maturing grapes. The sun is hot and the mountains too high for bugs to fly over them. Its Sauvignon Blanc is a light easy-drinking wine with lashings of grapefruit and lemon flavours.

Anyone who is looking for a partner to an assertive Stilton cheese will enjoy the 1985 Messias Port. It is a tawny port made with grapes from a single harvest which has been matured for at least seven years in a wooden cask. A pale, hazy copper red, its nose is full of Mediterranean fruits – oranges and figs. The intense finish is long and warming.

Made only with Malbec grapes, this Argentinian favourite from Mendoza is medium to full and rounded, bold without being over-assertive. A rich red-blue in colour, Malbec is one of the classic grapes of Burgundy. Its aroma exudes the warmth of a summer's day, with intriguing layers of pepper and fresh dark fruit. It has a long, warming finish, which cries out to be paired with red meat.

How the world of wine has changed. The Nandi Hills, just north of Bangalore in India, might not be most people's idea of a winemaking region, but it is. Grover has more than 100 hectares of vines and now even sells wine to France. La Réserve, a Cabernet Shiraz, is aged in French oak and is a powerful, luscious mix of dark plums and blackcurrants.

47 Villiers St,
City of London
WC2N 6NE
www.gordonswinebar.com

(All photos Cath Harries)

LE BEAUJOLAIS

Quirky, quaint and quintessentially Gallic.

Le Beaujolais takes its name from one of Burgundy's most famous winemaking regions. It has been a little piece of France in the heart of London since 1972.

Plus ça change, plus c'est la même chose – the more things change, the more things stay the same. While newer bars are showy, flashy and at the cutting edge of today's technology, this bar is outwardly and unashamedly stuck in the past.

Reputedly London's oldest French-run wine bar, Le Beaujolais has seemingly always been the same. It was probably new once, but has forever looked careworn. Small inside and with a ragbag set of furniture, it is a well-loved place with an eclectic and casual collection of wine labels, which hang from the ceiling or are stuck to the walls. There is also a display of ties, which were seemingly left by tipsy advertising executives and public schoolboys, from an era when all businessmen wore them.

It is a wholehearted, no frills Gallic bar, a moment away from the madness of Leicester Square, which is an engaging and enthralling London experience.

The plates of bread and cheese are evocative of happy days spent in France, frightened by the attitude of the waiters. The plates of sharing charcuteries are great fun.

Engaging, relaxed and welcoming, its dark, cosy and intimate atmosphere make it a good place to listen, talk and laugh with friends and occasionally listen to a bit of jazz and blues.

25 Litchfield Street, Leicester Square, WC2H 9NJ
www.lebeaujolais.london

Beaujolais Nouveau

The Beaujolais region is home to a style of wine, Beaujolais Nouveau, which became part of 1980s mythology in the UK.

It is a callow, immature wine made for early drinking. Gamay is the grape which predominates. It cannot be released to consumers until after midnight on the third Wednesday in November.

So, on the third Thursday of every November wine bars in the UK were awash with Beaujolais Nouveau celebrations. There was a fierce rivalry between bars to serve the light red wine, which was usually served well chilled, as early as possible.

The run began after wine writers Clement Freud and Joseph Berkmann had a bet in 1970 to see who could get bottles of the wine back to London first. The event caught on and across England wine bar managers and owners took part in Gumball Rally type races to get the first bottles of the new vintage back to the UK and on sale.

Bentleys, motorbikes and white vans all took part in the madcap dash from the south of France. One year a consignment arrived by Harrier jet.

It was a huge marketing success, but like much of the 1980s it didn't last long into the 1990s. Along with mobile phones the size of house bricks, eight-track stereos and jackets with padded shoulders its popularity waned.

Overhyped and overpriced, in the end much of the wine sold was of poor quality which didn't reflect well on the winemakers of Beaujolais.

Beaujolais Nouveau Day is still celebrated in Japan, which imports hundreds of hectolitres a year. Such is the excitement that many bathers choose to swim in it at the Hakone Yunessun spa in Hakone – though the liquid is mainly water and red dye and only contains nine litres of the wine. So there is no likelihood of getting drunk should you swallow the liquid and many children also enjoy frolicking in the water.

▶ The Hakone Yunessun spa in Japan contains a very small volume of wine.

(Hakone Yunessun)

28-50

Virtually all of the world's commercial vineyards in the northern and southern hemispheres are located between the latitudes of 28° and 50°, hence the bar's name. And not only do the staff seem to have drunk most of them, they can tell a story about each of them too.

However, rather than stock them all, there is an ever-changing range of 15 reds and 15 whites, with the promise that to try them is a journey of discovery highlighting wines from different regions and the attributes of different grapes.

For anyone wanting to know more about wine, 28-50 holds regular workshops for drinkers. Every month a winemaker showcases a range of his or her wines. Most of the wines will be available by the glass, including a special cuvée or vintage coming straight from the winery.

The restaurant with its excellent bistro style food can seat about 50, and 18 can get into the bar and pick at quality cheeses and charcuteries.

The chefs set the highest standards and have worked for many of the world's greatest food creators, including Anton Mosimann and Gordon Ramsay. The restaurant is normally busy without being overcrowded, loud but not deafening and of the highest quality without requiring a second mortgage to pay for it.

This is a modern retro bar which is worth seeking out. Some people might frown upon those who drink a couple of glasses of the world's greatest wines in a basement, at lunchtime, before walking up a flight of stairs into the daylight and clamour of Fetter Lane, but at 28-50 that is a life-affirming experience.

London is also home to two other 28-50 restaurant bars, which are owned by the same company; the others are in Marylebone and Mayfair.

140 Fetter Lane, City of London EC4A 1BT
www.2850.co.uk/fetter

1855

Oxford is indeed a city of dreaming spires and now it is home to 1855.

A newly opened, swish, stylish, smart bar, its name pays homage to one of the greatest events in French wine: the creation of the 1855 Classification of the red wines of the Gironde. This was the creation of Napoleon III for the 1855 Exposition Universelle in Paris, a major exhibition to highlight all good things French.

Bordeaux's leading wine brokers were asked to produce a list of the best wines in the region, grouped by quality into five levels called *crus* (growths). *Premier cru* (first growth) was the highest quality and fifth growth the lowest.

The dealers chose a method based on the price of the

▼ **Great wines at affordable prices are celebrated at 1855.**
(Cath Harries)

▲ **Easy-going and relaxed, 1855 is serious about its collection of wine.** (Cath Harries)

wine – the more expensive it was, the better its quality was assumed to be. The final list included 61 producers, with the best of the best, or in this case the most expensive, being from the Lafitte chateau.

The list has more or less stood the test of time – save for the addition of Château Cantemerle in 1856. A clerical error meant it was left off the original list. And in 1973, Château Mouton Rothschild was promoted from second to first growth status.

The 1855 classification was not the first that had been attempted. The American ambassador to France, Thomas Jefferson, had put together a list in the late 18th century. And last century several attempts were made to devise a new system, but the 1855 classification still continues to hold sway as being the quality list.

Quality also exudes from 1855's wine list, which is curated by wine expert Alistair Cooper.

He has shown a preference for wines which are made with minimal chemical intervention and the maximum commitment by the artisanal producers. Many of the wines, which are not confined to those just from France, are produced organically and bio-dynamically.

4 Oxford Castle, New Road, Oxford OX1 1AY.
www.1855oxford.com

▶ **Some of the world's most famous grape varieties can be found in bottles at 1855.** (Cath Harries)

BERRY BROS & RUDD

There's a comfortable, aged, elegance to Berry Bros & Rudd's shop in St James's in central London. It is calm, contented and composed.

A clock ticks, marking time, not just in minutes or moments but in wine vintages.

The family company has been trading at No. 3 St James's Street for more than three centuries.

It is a place where kings and princes, peers and politicians and ordinary folk have bought their wine. It all started in 1698, when the Widow Bourne opened a grocery store opposite St James's Palace – which became the official home of the monarch.

Now, after more than 315 years, it has a glorious history, some of which is displayed on the wall. It includes two Royal Warrants, the hiding of Napoleon III in the cellars, a telegram detailing 69 cases of wine and spirits supplied to the ill-fated *Titanic*, and the selling of liquor to smugglers in the Bahamas running alcohol into Prohibition-era America.

It has seen the French revolution, world wars, changes of monarchs and it is still flourishing.

And certainly George III (1760–1820) or people from his household shopped here, as it was he who gave the shop its first royal warrant.

The staff who worked here must have seen much change – today cars and lorries stop and start on the busy road outside and Lycra-clad cyclists flash by the window where 300 years ago crowds would gather for bearbaiting, cockfighting and duelling.

Over time the shop's business moved from groceries to coffee and it supplied some of St James's most fashionable

coffee shops. Today it still trades under the Sign of the Coffee Mill, an image that has remained outside the shop for centuries.

Standing inside the shop is a large weighing scale – it was installed sometime around the 1760s. It became fashionable for customers to be weighed at the Sign of the Coffee Mill. In the shop can be seen large red ledgers; the customers' weights are written in these books. Among the luminaries included are Lord Byron, Beau Brummel, William Pitt the Younger and the Aga Khan.

(All photos Cath Harries)

George Berry became involved in the business in 1803, and by 1810 his name was above the door. Over time the business evolved from coffee into wine and spirits.

Old it might be, venerable it certainly is – but there is something egalitarian about the shop. Yes, Chancellors of the Exchequer might shop here, as do some of Mayfair's finest looking for a bottle of Champagne to go with their lunch, but so do white-van driving builders, office workers and other ordinary folk looking for something to drink that night or a bottle to celebrate a special birthday or anniversary.

Today, Britain's oldest wine and spirit merchant is a vibrant, thriving business with trading links worldwide and a state of the art warehouse in Basingstoke.

'The initial trade was coffee, spices and tea', says the shop's manager Francis Huick, who started work here in 2005.

We are sitting in the Berry Bros parlour – a place unseen by most customers. It's small and intimate, with a glowing coal fire and a display of long-since empty wine bottles which date back to the 18th century.

Francis comes from Burgundy, and used to play with grapes as a child. 'I was a terrible kid and used to throw clusters of grapes at the pickers!' he confided.

'It is not an exact science to make wine – there is a lot of work in the vineyard to be done – it is from great grapes that good wines if not great wines come. And it all starts in the vineyard.

'When I drink a wine, I want to experience emotions. I can go two to six months without having a drink, but when I taste something I want to feel something inside.

'When tasting, I look for an emotion and experience – I want wine to transport me back to my youth, or back to where it comes from, I want something to happen. It can be a smell of a horse stable in Burgundy – there are smells you cannot forget, it can be smells of my mother cooking or the smell of the garden.

'Wine is able to gather people together, it is one of the greatest things we have in life – wine is made to be enjoyed.

'When tasting, sometimes we will write off a wine too quickly. We are too impatient. And there is nothing wrong in saying I disagree with someone else's interpretation of a wine.'

The fire burns in the grate, some smoke curls and circles away. Warming, it takes the chill from the room.

'There's a warming energy in good wine, you can taste it. When it's flat you can taste that too.' He shrugs his shoulders at the notion of celebrity winemakers.

'The most honest, humble producers always put themselves in the background – for them the wine must do the talking.

(All photos Cath Harries)

'There are others – some want to do too much. I want the wine to express itself.

'A wine doesn't have to be expensive to be great. It can come from a modest wine region – but it can be great – it can be cheap and be great.

'There are many wines that you might taste that are great because of the moment – the ambiance – it's a special instant.

'As human beings there are times when we need to enjoy something, because life can be quite tough. We need emotion, time and conversation.

'We need wine, it is like a car – you don't have to buy a Bentley, there's a wine for every budget and every moment.

'When you taste, don't go too quickly. You have to concentrate on the moment. I am not an expert, I prefer passion.

'Wine can be snobbish – it shouldn't be – people should have the humility.

'Wine can be complex – you must respect things. You have to understand and when you rush, you forget. Sometimes I think about a wine for two or three days – it helps me understand it.

'We have some of the finest wines in the world, but we also have wines for everyone.

'There is a joy to buying wine, there's a joy to looking at a bottle and thinking about it and there's the joy of drinking it. That's the excitement I look for.'

Here are half a dozen of Francis' favourite wines.

2012 Condrieu, Côteau de Vernon, Domaine Georges Vernay
The vines are tightly packed on to crowded granite stone terraces in the Rhône. The wine matures in wooden vats of different types for 18 months before being blended.

2010 Pouilly-Fumé, Silex, Didier Dagueneau
A complex wine, with a lot to talk about. It's opulent and engaging, a broad canvas of ripe fruits and citrus zest. Pure silk in a glass, its long finish resonates.

Domaine Pichard, Madiran Cuvée René
This is rich intensity in a glass. This is a wine for keeping. Dark and brooding, it reveals a soft gentle fruitiness. It's moreish, and mixes swathes of sugar and spice.

2005 Marqués de Haro, La Rioja
From a single vineyard, it's a fine example of the wine blender's art, bringing together Tempranillo and Graciano grapes and the complexities of French and American oak barrels.

2005 Hermitage, Domaine Jean-Louis Chave
A wine of some eminence and one of the best vintages. It is one which benefits from being given time when drinking it, and don't rush to conclusions. Take another sip and think again.

2003 Barolo Monprivato, Castiglione Falletto, Giuseppe Mascarello
Dark red fruits and mineral flavours clamour for attention. It is a full wine, with a strong personality. It's a wine to have a conversation with.

(All photos Cath Harries)

Bottling it up

So what's in a bottle? Quite a lot it seems. Thanks to European Union legislation 750ml is the most common size. But traditionally each of the major European wine regions developed their own style of bottle.

Historically, it's said the size of the bottle depended on the lung capacity of the glass blower. Well German blowers must have had a lot of puff, as one litre bottles were once popular. And in parts of France wine was put into a jeroboam, which could contain up to three litres. Now that's some puff.

Over time wine bottles have come in many different shapes and sizes. But they all have a mouth, neck, shoulder or ogive and a bottom. The bottom could be flat or have an indentation known as a punt.

To some the punt is an essential attribute of Bordeaux and Burgundy bottles, as it allows the yeast and other elements of any sediment to be collected in the bottle rather than being poured into the glass. Others say a punt make the bottle stronger and easier to transport.

In reality it's probably a throwback to the early day of bottle making, when some glass blowers would attach a wooden stick known as a pontil to the base of a bottle as it was being blown. The stick left an indentation. And the rest they say is tradition.

Many winemakers will tell you that the particular attributes of the bottles they use contribute to the character of the wines they contain. It is hard to prove such statements, however, one thing is certain, such views all add to the fun of wine.

There are three basic bottle shapes: skinny, strapping and sensuously shapely. Or, as wine experts will tell you, from Germany come the winsome tall bottles as favoured by winemakers in the Alsace. Just think Riesling. There's a swagger to big-shouldered bottles with a pronounced punt from Bordeaux. And look out for the sashay of bottles of Cabernet or Merlot. Bordeaux makers say the shoulders were developed to capture sediment produced by their highly tannic wines.

And then there are the voluptuous, low-shouldered bottles found in Burgundy. The softer, less tannic Pinot Noirs favoured by the region's winemakers apparently don't need the high shoulders as the wines don't have as much sediment.

The Tuscany region of Italy gives us another bottle style: Chianti. Traditionally it was a squat bottle wrapped in a straw basket.

Champagne and other sparkling wine bottles are beefier brothers of Bordeaux bottles. The heavy weight of the glass is needed to withstand the pressure of the carbonated wine wanting to explode out. There's a lot of carbon dioxide in a bottle of the bubbles – equivalent to 5–6 atmospheres of pressure. Now that's some gas.

(Cath Harries)

Wine bottle sizes

- **Split – 187ml.**
- **Half-bottle – 375ml, or one half of the standard bottle size.**
- **Bottle – 750ml, the standard size.**
- **Magnum – Two bottles or 1.5 litres.**
- **Double magnum – Twice the size of a magnum, holding three litres, or the equivalent of four bottles.**
- **Jeroboam – Just to be confusing, there are two sizes of Jeroboams: the sparkling wine Jeroboam holds four bottles, or three litres; the still wine Jeroboam holds six regular bottles, or 4.5 litres.**
- **Rehoboam – Champagne only – 4.5 litres or six bottles.**
- **Imperial – Holds six litres or the equivalent of eight bottles. Tends to be Bordeaux shaped.**
- **Methuselah – Same size as an Imperial (six litres), but is generally used for sparkling wines and is Burgundy-shaped.**
- **Salmanazar – Holds 12 bottles or nine litres.**
- **Balthazar – Holds 16 bottles or 12 litres.**

Spiritual wine

It is not easy to explain the science of biodynamic viticulture. But, it is the buzzword of some of today's most creative and innovative winemakers.

Biodynamics takes organic farming to a more spiritual, ethereal level. The father of the movement is widely regarded as being Austrian philosopher Rudolf Steiner who gave a series of lectures in 1924 setting out the broad principles.

Biodynamics is much more than an agricultural system, it is a philosophy, which has some similarities with Gaia philosophy developed by author James Lovelock.

The Lovelock idea, which was named after Gaia, the Greek goddess of the earth, it is a broadly inclusive term for related concepts that suggest living organisms on a planet will affect the nature of their environment in order to make the environment more suitable for life.

To farm biodynamically, first you have to think biodynamically, as it impacts on growing grapes in a number of ways.

Steiner, before he developed his theory on agriculture, wanted to bring together the material and spiritual worlds through the philosophical method. To this end, he created the spiritual science of anthroposophy.

It was only quite late on in Steiner's life that he turned to agriculture. His seminal lectures, entitled Spiritual Foundations for the Renewal of Agriculture, were delivered just a year before his death, but they remain as ideas underpinning biodynamic farming.

Key to biodynamics is considering the vineyard as a living, self-sustaining system, which is nurtured by lunar and cosmic rhythms. The terroir is much more than a medium in which the vines grow, it is a living organism in its own right.

Biodynamic growers do not use synthetic fertilizers or pesticides. Instead they apply a series of seemingly weird preparations, which are utilised in keeping with the rhythms and cadences of nature. True biodynamic growers follow the moon's cycles.

Disease is seen as a sign of a malaise with the terroir or organism of the vineyard. Deal with the problem in the system and the disease will right itself.

The idea has gained traction among many grape growers around the world some of whom are certified as biodynamic growers, others of whom follow the movement's broad principles, saying that it is a philosophy rather than a strict set of rules.

Loosely, biodynamics can be broken down into the a number of areas, including two field sprays derived from cow horn, five or six compost preparations that deliver healing herbs added to the compost, and the use of a planting calendar that gives clear indications as to when to carry out tasks in the vineyard.

One of the most common preparations is derived from the horsetail, a plant usually regarded as a weed, which is said

▲ **Potions made from fermented cow manure and horn, are used to vitalise the ground.** (Biodynamic Association)

▼ **Unwanted by most gardeners, horsetail, or marestail, is used to inhibit the growth of unwanted funguses.** (Cath Harries)

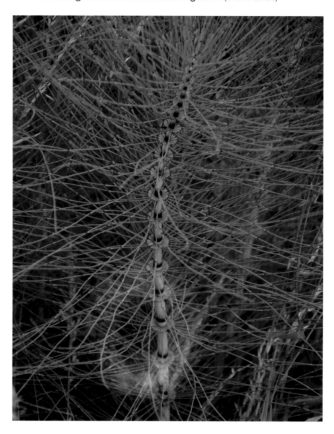

to control unwanted funguses and drive them back into the soil. Moist, warm weather in the days following a full moon are most likely to encourage mildews and the development of blight and other fungi. According to proponents of biodynamics, horsetail is very rich in silica, and silica has a strong connection with light. This makes it an ideal antidote to the darkness-loving fungus world.

The spray preparations, or field sprays, are made from cow manure and quartz meal, and are known as horn manure and horn silica. Horn manure is cow manure that has been fermented in the soil over the winter inside a cow horn. Horn silica is finely ground quartz meal that spends the summer in the soil inside a cow horn.

Before being applied very small amounts, these prepared substances are dissolved in water and stirred vigorously for one whole hour, preferably by hand, until a deep vortex is formed in the stirring vessel. Then the direction is changed, the liquid seethes, and slowly a new vortex is formed. Each time a well-formed vortex is achieved, the direction is changed until the hour is up.

Another preparation involves dandelion flowers fermented in a cow's intestines.

Strange it all might sound, but one thing cannot be denied – some biodynamically grown grapes do make superb wines.

▼ **Roses grown at the end of vines act as early warning of mildew, a fungal disease.** (Cath Harries)

(Cath Harries)

Have tastes in wine changed over the generations?

Climate change is altering the tastes of wine drinkers, encouraging them to prefer intense, higher alcohol wines, according to research by Naked Wines.

Research by the online wine retailer suggests that our tastes are changing because of climate change.

It seems we are enjoying more wines from hotter climes and are moving up the strength scale, with many preferring their favourite wine to be above 14% ABV.

The research found people showed a growing preference for punchier, more intense wines with a higher alcohol content, compared to 20 or 30 years ago.

The findings have been based on data collected from Naked Wines' customers over a seven-year period, having analysed three million ratings on more than 1,700 wines.

Naked Wines' wine director, Ray O'Connor, said: 'The impact of modern viticulture and winemaking has seen vines become more efficient, meaning they produce greater sugar levels, resulting in higher alcohol.

'Despite the long-term challenges that climate change can have on wine regions around the world, presently the short-term benefit is that producers are making more consumer-friendly wines.'

It seems that moderate increases in temperature over the growing season deliver riper fruit, greater intensity, and higher sugar levels to the wine, which seems to be exactly what people are wanting.

'While there is no doubt that climate change will make winemaking a challenge in the long term, the short-term effects in some regions are actually appealing to current tastes,' said O'Connor.

CHAPTER 5
WINEMAKING

(Cath Harries)

From the vine to the glass

Wine is a simple drink with great complexity and usually, all you need is grapes.

The winemaker extracts the juice from the grapes and waits. Usually yeast will be added to the juice, however, sometimes wild yeast will undertake its mysterious work; either way, the fermentation process begins.

Once the yeast has finished converting the sugar in the grape juice into carbon dioxide and alcohol, we have wine – well, nearly.

The wine will now be allowed to condition or mature before it is put into a bottle.

It is such a simple process. However, without the skill of the winemaker, whether at home or in a commercial winery, none of it would happen .

Commercial winemaking

The process of turning grapes into wine is not quite as old as time, but it is likely that if an ancient was suddenly transported into one of today's wineries he or she would find that while some of the techniques might have changed, the overall process is much the same.

Grapes are grown, harvested, squashed to get the juice out and then fermented.

Of course all winemakers will have their own idiosyncrasies, but this is part of what makes wines different from region to region and winery to winery. Indeed, long live the differences – they give wines their personalities and complexities.

It all begins with the grapes. Each vineyard is likely to have its own vinification process – some crush the grapes before fermentation, others throw whole bunches, stalks and all into the fermenting vessels.

Broadly speaking most red wines will be macerated before fermentation. Some winemakers add yeast, others let the yeasts naturally present on the grape skins ferment the juice.

To begin with all grape juice is clear, but red wine takes its colour from the juice coming into contact with grape skins and pips which add colour and tannins. The grape skins and other residues are known as the pomace. This usually forms a cap on top of the fermenting wine and the winemaker will daily break it up and push it into the juice, so that it comes in contact with more of the juice.

When the fermentation is finished, the wine is placed in barrels or vats for maturation. During this time most red wines and even some white wines undergo a malolactic fermentation – this is what gives some Chardonnays a buttery taste. No alcohol is made during a malolactic fermentation, instead, bacteria turn malic acid into the smoother tasting lactic acid.

However, whether for red, white or rosé wine, the first thing to do is to pick the grapes.

(Wines of Argentina)

MAKING RED WINE

1 Destem and crush the grapes
This breaks the skins of the juice and releases the juice.

(Burgundy Tourism)

2 Vatting/maceration
Everything, the whole lot – juice, skins, and even some stalks – are put into a tank or vat for maceration. Colour and tannins pass from the skins into the juice.

3 Cap punching
The pomace (cap of skins) is broken up and pushed into the juice; in France the process is sometimes called pigeage. The juice will frequently be pumped back over the pomace top when it has reformed.

4 Fermentation
Yeast, either from the grape skins or added separately, begins to get to work. As part of its lifecycle it converts the sugars into carbon dioxide gas and creates, thankfully for us, a waste product which we call alcohol.

5 Running off
With the fermentation complete, the free-run wine goes into a tank or barrel. The marc (the debris at the bottom of the container) is removed.

(Burgundy Tourism)

6 Pressing
The marc is pressed and the juice which runs off can be used for blending into the wine. In some places it is distilled into a grape-based spirit.

7 Malolactic fermentation
Micro-organisms in the wine turn the malic acid in the grapes into lactic acid, giving off CO_2 and slightly reducing the acidity. The lactic acid created makes the wine smoother, creates tannins and some say gives a dairy, buttery taste. A malolactic fermentation is not the same as a secondary fermentation as no alcohol is created.

8 Racking
Some winemakers will move the wine to another container and add sulphite to prevent further microbiological activity. It stops the wine going off.

(Wines of Argentina)

9 Maturing
The wine will be left to mature, usually in large wooden barrels. This adds further flavours to the wine.

10 Blending
The wine is blended into a tank and the sulphite level adjusted.

11 Fining
A fining, a clearing agent, is added. It could be egg white, which draws any impurities to the bottom of the tank.

12 Filtering and bottling
The wine may now be filtered; it is then bottled, corked or capped and labelled.

MAKING WHITE WINE

For many white wines the grapes are pressed straight after harvesting, usually without destalking. The liquid will be separated from the skins and other debris. The juice is put into a barrel or a vat and fermentation begins.

1 Pressing/vatting
The grapes are crushed in a large press, releasing the cloudy juice known as must, which is pumped or poured into a large tank.

2 Must settling/racking
The cloudy juice or must is allowed to settle. This can happen naturally or enzymes might be added to speed up the process. Once cleared the liquid is run off into another barrel or vessel.

3 Alcoholic fermentation/racking
Yeast will be added to the must and fermentation will occur. When it is complete the wine will be racked.

4 Second (malolactic) fermentation
Some white wines, particularly Chardonnay, undergo a malolactic fermentation as explained earlier for red wine.

5 Racking/sulphiting
Some winemakers will add sulphite to prevent spoilage.

6 Maturing
The wine will be stored in large wooden or metal vats to mature, a process which could take from 8 to 18 months, sometimes longer. This helps develop the wine's character. If the wine is being matured on lees, it is stirred to keep the fine particles in suspension.

7 Blending
The wine is put into a tank and blended as required.

8 Fining
A fining (clearing) agent such as egg white can be added to help clear the wine. The particles collect at the bottom of the barrel. There are many winemakers who choose not to add finings.

9 Filtration/bottling
Usually, the wine will be filtered before bottling, corking or capping and labelling.

MAKING A ROSÉ WINE

The must is run off from the skins after only a few hours, so only small amounts of tannins and colours are taken up in the must. It is then fermented and matured as a red wine.

Making wine at home is easy

Making your own wine is easy and fun to do. Most of the equipment for your first vintage can be found in a normal kitchen – running water and some containers will do for starters – but it's much easier with the addition of some extra bits and pieces that can easily be bought from a local home winemaking shop or on the internet.

STARTER KITS

These juice kits come complete with every ingredient needed to start your home winemaking journey. The kits normally come in two sizes to make 6 or 30 bottles of your very own wine. They are quick and easy and you can be drinking your first wine in a matter of days.

FRUIT CONCENTRATE

Once starter kits have been mastered, it can be fun to go on to the next stage, making wine from cans of concentrate. There is a huge variety of grape concentrates available. In addition, should you tire of grapes, you can try concentrates of other fruits such as blackberries or peaches.

You need good grapes to make the very best wines, but a good way to learn about winemaking, the attributes of different grapes and wine styles is to start with a wine kit. The result is likely to be pretty drinkable. And once you have mastered the techniques many winemakers move on and make wine from grapes.

Wine kits allow the home winemaker to source grapes from California, Australia, Portugal, Spain or Italy at any time of the year. The kits also allow the maker to experience different styles of grape – be they late harvest, ports, sherries, sparkling or ice wines.

There are four main types of wine kits: pure juice; fully concentrated grape juice; partially concentrated grape juice; combined juice and concentrate. Providing you follow the instructions, all are easy to use.

The process will take longer than using a starter kit. The primary fermentation will take about a week. The wine will then be racked into a secondary fermenter and over a two-month period it is likely to be racked several more times.

MAKING WINE FROM WHOLE FRUIT

Most people regard this as the ultimate form of home winemaking. The fermentable material doesn't come in a can. You will have to prepare the fruit for fermentation yourself. You will also have to choose which wine yeast you will want to use. A little bit of science will be useful, but it's not essential. But the principles learnt with a starter kit will still hold good – cleanliness, and time and temperature control, are the basis of all good winemaking.

(All photos Cath Harries)

Things you need for making six bottles of wine from a starter kit

- A starter all-in-one wine kit
- Two fermentation containers (typically a 4.5 litre demijohn and a plastic bucket)
- A fermentation airlock
- A plastic funnel
- A siphon tube – approx 2m
- Measuring jug
- Large plastic spoon for stirring
- Sterilising solution
- Campden tablets
- Six empty glass wine bottles with corks or screw caps
- Hydrometer and a trial jar
- Heating belt or pad
- Finings
- Filter pads
- Thermometer
- A place to ferment the wine.

Why

- Two fermentation vessels – One to ferment in, another to siphon the fermented wine into.
- Airlock – It allows the release of carbon dioxide created during fermentation and stops air coming into contact with the wine.
- Hydrometer – To check when the fermentation process is finished.
- Siphon tube – To transfer the wine from one container to another, and finally into the bottles.
- Sterilising solution – To clean and sterilise all the equipment.
- Heating pad or belt – A warm, constant temperature is best for fermenting the wine. A heating belt or pad can achieve this.

A typical wine kit will contain

- A bottle or can of concentrated grape juice.
- Yeast nutrient.
- Oak chips – if it's a red wine.
- Stabiliser.
- A sachet of grape character concentrate.
- Finings.

Why

- Grape concentrate – The wine will be made from this.
- Yeast nutrient – Starts the fermentation process.
- Oak chips – Add barrel-ageing characteristics to the wine.
- Stabiliser – This stops the fermentation process.
- Grape character concentrate – This enhances the varietal characteristics of the wine.
- Finings – Will clear the wine.

TIPS FOR A SUCCESSFUL WINE

- Plan in advance where you will make your wine and what you will do.
- Cleanliness is essential to good winemaking. Unwanted bugs and microbes love the warm, sugary mixture you'll create. Make sure all the equipment is thoroughly cleaned, preferably with a good disinfectant or steriliser, then rinsed with clean water.

- Once fermentation has finished and the wine has been siphoned into bottles, thoroughly clean the fermentation vessel. Delay and you risk contaminating future fermentations.
- Be patient, try to leave the wine to mature for as long as the recipe says – this will help improve the quality.

STEP-BY-STEP GUIDE TO MAKING WINE FROM A CONCENTRATE KIT

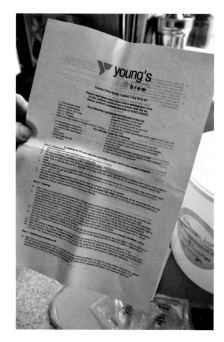

1 Get reading. Read and reread the instructions and familiarise yourself with the components and equipment. All kits follow similar principles, but details may vary.

2 Always thoroughly wash and sterilise all the equipment, even if it's brand new.

3 Boil water and allow to cool to 53°C.

4 Pour one litre of the hot water into the fermentation vessel and add 900g of sugar.

5 Stir to dissolve the sugar.

6 Add concentrate. Add the grape juice concentrate to the fermenting vessel and stir for 10 seconds. Rinse out the concentrate bottle or can using a small amount of tap water and add this to the container.

7 Add water. Add about three litres of cold tap water to the vessel. Stir for 20 seconds.

8 Add yeast and yeast nutrient. Take care to follow the instructions.

9 Add the oak chips and stir for 10 seconds.

10 Transfer the liquid to a demijohn. Fit the airlock and bung. Half fill the airlock with water and insert it into the bung to seal the vessel.

11 Keep in a warm place (20° to 25°C), or use a heating pad or belt. A bubbling, vibrant fermentation should begin within 24 hours. For this kit fermentation will take six days. Some kits take longer.

12 If you want to be sensible, place the fermentation vessel on a tray or similar. This will collect any excessive frothing.

13 After six days it is important to de-gas the wine. The easiest way to do this is to transfer the wine from one container to another at least six times. The second container should have been washed with hot water.

(All photos Cath Harries)

14 Check the liquid with the hydrometer. Take hydrometer readings at various stages to check on the remaining sugar level. For a dry wine: 0.990–0.996. Medium: 0.996–1.009. Sweet: 1.009–1.018. For this kit the specific gravity should be 0.994 or lower.

15 Fermentation can take longer than six days if the temperature has fallen below 20°C. Do not move to the next stage until the fermentation has finished.

16 Once the specific gravity is at 0.994, pour in one packet of stabiliser and stir for about 30 seconds.

17 Add the sachet which contains the varietal character concentrate and stir.

18 Pour in the finings and stir. Leave to stand for an hour.

19 Add more stabiliser and leave to stand for 24 hours. Leave the container on a work surface to allow later siphoning.

20 After 24 hours the wine should be clear. If not, be patient and give it another day. To check for clarity, siphon off a glass from halfway down the container. Hold it up and check it is clear. If it is not clear let it stand for another day.

21 Once clear, siphon the wine into the other cleaned container. It is important to siphon off as much as possible without disturbing the sediment at the bottom of the container. If any of the sediment is disturbed, pour any siphoned wine back into the original container and leave the sediment to re-settle for another 24 hours.

22 If you wish to sweeten the wine, it should be done at this stage. When sweetening, add one dessertspoon of sugar, stir to dissolve then taste. Repeat until the desired level of sweetness is achieved.

23 Finally, thoroughly rinse and sterilise six wine bottles and stoppers. Siphon the wine into the bottles, leaving about 5cm of space at the top, and seal. Some kits might ask you to filter the wine before it goes into the bottles. Fit the corks with a corking tool. To enhance appearance, fit labels.

(All photos Cath Harries)

MAKING WINE WITH REAL GRAPES

Whatever kind of grapes you use, the general techniques, equipment and ingredients are the same. Here's an overview of some key steps along the way.

Inspecting the fruit

Winemaking starts with inspecting the grapes. Make sure they are ripe by squishing up a good double handful, straining the juice and measuring the sugar level with a hydrometer, a handy device you can buy at a winemaking supply shop. The sugar density should be around 22° Brix.

The grapes also must be clean, sound and relatively free of insects and other vineyard debris. Discard any grapes that look rotten or otherwise suspicious. Also, it's very important that all the stems are removed, since they will make your wine bitter.

Keeping it clean

Winemaking demands a clean environment. Wash all of your equipment thoroughly with hot water, boiling what you can.

Adjusting the acidity

Adjusting the acidity of the juice or must of your wine is critical. Thankfully, it's also easy. Acid content is measured with a simple titration kit; you can buy one at a winemaking supply shop. The ideal acid level is 6 to 7 grams per litre for dry reds and 6.5 to 7.5 grams per litre for dry whites.

So, if the must measures 5.5 grams per litre, then you need to add 1 gram per litre of tartaric acid to bring it up to 6.5g/l. Add this powder in very small amounts, checking acidity after each addition, until the desired level is reached.

Red or white wines

Red wines are always fermented with the skins and pulp in the plastic pail; the solids are pressed after fermentation is complete. White wines are always pressed before fermentation, so only the grape juice winds up in the fermenting pail.

Home-grown grapes

If you are growing your own vines, before picking the grapes to make wine, make sure they are as ripe as possible. If the weather has been cold and wet it is possible that the grapes will be low in sugar and high in acidity. The juice may need a little sugar added to boost the specific gravity (SG) and it may be necessary to reduce the acidity by some degree. If the weather has been very good it may be that the grapes are sweet and lack a little acid. This can also be adjusted.

Making white wine

Typically 7 to 9kg of grapes will produce 4.5l of wine.

1 Place the open nylon straining bag into a sterilised bucket, put the grapes (no stalks) into the straining bag, crush the grapes and squeeze out the juice.
2 Stir in one teaspoon of pectic enzyme per 4.5l of juice.
3 Pour the juice into a demijohn (plastic or glass) or other fermenting vessel. Dispose of the now unwanted pulp.
4 Check the specific gravity reading and adjust to 1.080 with sugar if necessary.
5 Add the yeast and nutrient to the fermenting vessel. Fit a bung and airlock (half fill the airlock with water), then leave in a warm place at about 20°C until fermentation is complete.
6 When the fermentation ceases, check the specific gravity with the hydrometer. It should read 1.000 – this indicates that the wine is medium dry (not sweet).
7 Move to a cool place and after two to three days rack into a clean sterilised demijohn, leaving any sediment behind.
8 Further racking with the addition of Campden tablets will be necessary to remove sediment.
9 When the wine is clear, leave for two weeks then add a wine stabiliser (Potassium sorbate) with the Campden tablets.
10 If glass vessels are used, the wine can be left for four weeks or more before bottling. If plastic demijohns are used, bottle after two weeks.

Variations

According to the Home Brew Shop it is quite in order to add other fruits to the wine so as to produce a slightly different flavour – for instance, try adding 350g of gooseberries per 4.5l to the grapes.

5g per gallon of dried elderflowers can be added to the demijohn at the start to produce the bouquet and flavour of Liebfraumilch/Niersteiner style wine.

If you find your wine finishes too dry, use a liquid wine sweetener to sweeten to your taste, one bottle at a time. The remaining bottles can be left for those who prefer their wine on the dry side.

Making red wine

The process is similar to white wine. The main difference is that the pulp in the straining bag is left in contact with the juice while the initial fermentation takes place.

Variations

Try adding 250g of blackberries, elderberries or blackcurrants per 4.5l to the grapes.

With thanks to the Home Brew Shop, Aldershot (www.the-home-brew-shop.co.uk).

Growing in most people's gardens are the ingredients with which you can make some fabulous wines. And this step by step guide shows you how easy it is to do.

1 Prepare the fruit

If making wine from cherries or something similar remove the pits. But be careful not to use too much muscle or be tempted to throw everything into a food processor. Skin and seeds add unwanted bitterness to the wine and also make it harder to clear.

2 Get mixing and stirring

Put all the ingredients into the primary fermenting vessel and stir. But don't add the yeast yet. Put any pulp into a nylon bag and immerse into the mixture. Add water to fill the vessel. Add some Campden powder or tablets as instructed. The chemicals in the Campden compound have to do their work before the yeast can be added.

3 Covering up the must

Take a clean cloth and cover the fermenting vessels and wait for 24 hours. This is the time when the Campden compound is doing its necessary work. The must is being sterilised. Wild yeasts are all around us and they will be killed off too. Chlorine and chloramine, which are present in tap water, will also be eliminated.

4 Now you can add the yeast

Add the wine yeast as instructed. Usually this will mean sprinkling the powdered yeast over the surface of the must. Once again cover with the clean cloth. The yeast now needs to start to do its work, which will usually take from five to seven days. The first day is critical and you should see bubbling and foaming begin.

(All photos Cath Harries)

6 Fitting the airlock

Attach the airlock and half fill with some water. Allow the wine to continue to ferment for a further four to six weeks, or until it becomes completely clear. Time is of the essence: the longer the wine is left, the clearer it should be.

5 Transfer to the second fermenter

After five to seven days, remove the pulp from the fermenter. Squeeze out any residual juice back into the container. Siphon the wine into a fermenter which can be fitted with an airlock. You want to get as much liquid out as possible and it doesn't matter if a small amount of sediment is transferred. If needed, top the fermenter up with water.

7 Once clear, fill the bottles

Once the wine is crystal clear, siphon it off the sediment into another vessel. Be careful to ensure no sediment is siphoned off, you want to leave it behind. Add further Campden tablets or powder as instructed and fill the bottles. You may also adjust the sweetness of the wine at this stage, then siphon it into clean bottles and cork or cap them.

SOME SUITABLE FRUIT FOR WINEMAKING

Fruit	How much fruit (kg)		How much sugar (kg)		Extra fruit
	22.5 Litres	4.5 Litres	22.5 Litres	4.5 Litres	
Apple (Sour)	10	2	6.5	1.3	100g per 4.5 Litres of Blueberries
Blackcurrant	4	0.8	6.5	1.3	400g per 4.5 Litres of Redcurrants
Blackberry	6	1.2	6.5	1.3	100g per 4.5 Litres of Blueberries
Cherry (Black or Red)	10	2	6.5	1.3	100g per 4.5 Litres of Blueberries
Crab Apple	10	2	6.5	1.3	200g per 4.5 Litres of Raisins
Damson	10	2	6.5	1.3	Nothing Else
Elderberry	4	0.8	6.5	1.3	400g per 4.5 Litres of Raisins
Gooseberry	7	1.4	6.5	1.3	100g per 4.5 Litres of Blueberries
Greengage	10	2	6.5	1.3	150g per 4.5 Litres of Raisins
Loganberry	4	0.8	6.5	1.3	200g per 4.5 Litres of Blueberries
Pear	8	1.6	6.5	1.3	Nothing Else
Plum	8	1.6	6.5	1.3	150g per 4.5 Litres of Raisins
Raisin	4	0.8	6.5	1.3	Nothing Else
Raspberry	4	0.8	6.5	1.3	150g per 4.5 Litres of Raisins
Redcurrant	4	0.8	7.5	1.5	400g per 4.5 litres of Blackcurrants
Rosehip	0.5	0.1	6.5	1.3	150g per 4.5 Litres of Raisins
Rowanberry	5	1	6.5	1.3	300g per 4.5 Litres of Raisins
Strawberry	5	1	6.5	1.3	120g per 4.5 litres of Raisins

E C Kraus

GETTING INTO A FERMENT – YEAST

Yeast is all around us. From ancient times through most of history, winemakers knew that some form of transformation was taking place, transforming grape juice into wine. Wine must have been made in this way for many hundreds of years – the unknown and indeed unseen yeast was eating the sugar in must and converting it to carbon dioxide and alcohol.

Without yeast, there would be no wine. Starter wine kits usually come with their own yeast. But as people get more advanced in their winemaking, they have the opportunity to choose the yeast appropriate to the style of wine being made.

However, whatever yeast you choose, you probably won't be able to exclude the contribution of the wild yeasts which live naturally on grapes. Once the alcohol level reaches 5% most of these wild yeasts will die.

Choosing yeast

Yeast selection is of prime importance to the winemaker. Once the winemaker wants to move on from self-contained kits, decisions about the amount of fruit, the sugar content of the must and the strain of yeast used will have to be made.

Yeast for home winemakers generally comes in two types, liquid and dried. Dried yeasts are easy to use, cheap and they have a much longer shelf life than liquid yeasts, but the choice of dried yeast strains is very limited in comparison to liquid and some say they do not have such a great depth of flavour.

Liquid yeasts require refrigeration, have a limited shelf life and are more expensive. There is a huge range which gives the winemaker great scope for experimenting. Although liquid yeasts are more expensive, they can easily be reused by storing some from a primary fermentation in a sterilised jar in the fridge for a couple of weeks before using again in a new fermentation.

The most common strains of yeast used for winemaking come from the Saccharomyces cerevisiae family. They are relatively easy to use and over the years have been refined so that they thrive in wine.

(Cath Harries)

So how do you decide which yeast to use?

Like it or not, it is the yeast that contributes the most to any wine you want to make. For it is the microorganism which will transform your grapes or other fruit into a drink of sublime perfection – if all goes well.

It is the yeast that creates the alcohol which contains many of the flavour and aroma components of a wine. And different yeasts work better for some styles of wine, perform best at different temperatures and some prefer different types of grapes.

So you have to ask yourself what type of wine are you trying to make – red, white, dry, sweet, full-bodied or sparkling? Is it going to be a sherry style or port wine?

Most home winemaking shops stock a wide range of different yeasts – each with a different specification.

People who make beer at home are probably more creative in the types of yeast they use. Winemakers up to now have tended to be more conservative – nothing wrong with that in itself – but it is a little like living in a house with ten rooms and only using one of them, you are missing out on so much.

What type of wine do you want to make?
Each yeast strain has evolved and been cultured to work with specific varieties of grape. A yeast which is favoured for making white wines will bring out lighter, fruitier flavours. A red wine yeast is likely to produce alcohol with a big mouthfeel, a higher level of tannins and can even affect the colour of the wine.

Know your fermentation temperature
Different yeasts prosper at different temperatures. As a general rule white wines often ferment at a lower temperature than red. Trying to use a yeast at the wrong temperature is likely to result in a stuck fermentation.

How strong do you want the wine to be?
Some strains of yeast work better in wines which will have a final alcohol of 12% ABV; another strain will be needed if a 14% wine is wanted. If you are making a port wine, which could be up to 18% alcohol, a yeast strain which can tolerate this level of strength will be needed.

How fast is the fermentation?
If the yeast strain chosen ferments too quickly or too slowly unpleasant side effects can result. One of the most common is the production of smells like bad eggs – hydrogen sulphide.

Higher temperatures are likely to result in faster fermentations, but this can also stress some yeast strains, which will impart some unwanted flavour compounds.

Foaming ferments
Some fermentations can become extremely messy and overflow the container into which the must has been put. Some yeasts produce more foam than others, but they could be ideal for the style of wine you are wanting to make. It is

always best to put higher foaming yeast into larger, over-capacity vessels. It'll save a lot of mess.

Fermenting flocculation

Fermentation results in the creation of a lot of sediment and little pieces of protein and lots of dead yeast cells floating in the must. Different yeasts flocculate (settle out) in different ways. Too much flocculation can result in wine being wasted. A wine which is going to be drunk within a year will need a yeast strain which settles out very quickly.

Acid and other chemicals

Fermentation creates volatile acids – such as acetic acid. Volatile acids are usually good in small quantities. If the yeast creates too much, quality can be affected and the wine becomes spoiled. Acetaldehyde is a by-product of alcoholic fermentation and can add complexity to a wine.

Another consideration in choosing a yeast strain is its compatibility with malolactic bacteria and a malolactic fermentation. If you are looking for a malolactic fermentation then choose a yeast which is compatible with the bacteria.

Feeding the yeast

Even though there should be enough fermentable material and nutrients in most must to enable the yeast to thrive, sometimes the yeast needs feeding. Poor grapes or unripe fruits will be low on nutrients to feed the yeast. A must with very high levels of sugars can also be low in nutrients.

Quick summary to choosing a yeast

- Make sure the yeast strain matches the variety of grapes being used.
- What style of wine do you want to make?
- What are the fruits like – ripe, overripe or not yet ripe?
- Don't just choose a generic yeast strain – one which is specific for the wine being made will usually be the best.

There are many strains of yeast and companies which supply them. A good winemaking shop will offer advice on the best.

Some of the best known suppliers of yeast include: Wyeast, White Labs and Lallemand – though others are available.

Examples of yeast strains

Wyeast strain 4021 for dry white/sparkling wines

Used in many white wine fermentations and also some red wines. Ferments crisp and dry, ideal for base wines in making sparkling wine. Low foaming, excellent barrel fermentation, good flocculating characteristics.

- Attenuation: Not available
- Flocculation: Medium
- Temperature range: 13° to 24°C
- Alcohol tolerance: up to 17% ABV

Wyeast 4028 for Red™

Ideal for red or white wines which mature rapidly with Beaujolais type fruitiness, and for bigger reds requiring ageing. Low foaming, low sulphur production over a broad range of temperatures.

- Attenuation: Not available
- Flocculation: Medium-high
- Temperature range: 13° to 32°C
- Alcohol tolerance: 14% ABV

White Labs WLP700 – for sherry

It develops a flor on the surface of the wine. Creates green almond, Granny Smith and nougat characteristics found in sherry. Can also be used for port, Madeira and other sweet styles.

- Attenuation: >80%
- Flocculation: Not available
- Temperature range: >21°C
- Alcohol tolerance: 16% ABV

White Labs WLP Steinberg-Geisenheim

Ideal for fruity German wines, it produces good examples of Riesling and Gewürztraminer. It is cold tolerant.

- Attenuation: >80%
- Flocculation: Low
- Temperature range: 10° to 32°C
- Alcohol tolerance: 14% ABV

Lallemand Lalvin BM4X4

Good for most red and white wines, but not so good for a rosé.

- Attenuation: Not available
- Flocculation: Moderate
- Temperature range: 16° to 28°C
- Alcohol tolerance: 16% ABV

(Cath Harries)

Home winemaking – troubleshooting

Symptom	Possible causes	Reason and solutions
Fermentation has failed to start		
■ No bubbles or froth on the surface of the must ■ No characteristic fermentation odour ■ No activity through the airlock	■ Must too cold (yeast dormant) ■ Must too hot (yeast stunned/killed) ■ Old yeast (expired check best before date) ■ The lid and/or the airlock of the fermenter are not adequately sealing or not screwed down tight enough ■ Forgot to add the yeast	■ Give it a bit of time – allow at least twelve hours between the addition of yeast and the first active signs of fermentation before you do anything. ■ Pitching the yeast into must that is too cold or allowed to become too cold may prevent fermentation or significantly slow down fermentation. Move the fermenter to a warmer place (18° to 23°C) and rouse the yeast by stirring the must with a sterilised spoon. ■ Pitching yeast into must that is too hot (>35°C) or allowed to become too hot may kill or stun the yeast resulting in slow or no fermentation. Move the fermenter to a cooler place. When the must has cooled sufficiently (18° to 24°C) stir in another sachet of yeast. ■ Dried yeast has a finite life and can lose its viability with time especially if exposed to the air or moisture. Always ensure the sachet of yeast is within the best before date and not damaged. Always store yeast sachets in a cool, dry place. Stir in a new sachet of yeast. ■ If the airlock and/or fermenter lid is not sealed then there will be no active bubbling through the airlock. The must may actually be fermenting, but the CO_2 gas will be escaping through the faulty seal. Fermentation can be verified by removing the fermenter lid and examining the must. Indicators of fermentation are: condensation inside the lid, frothing/bubbling of the surface of the must and a ring of scum on the fermenter wall above the must. Rectify the faulty seal. Ensure fermenter lid is pushed down tightly. ■ The must contains too much sugar and the yeast has been inhibited. Dilute with water until the SG is below 1.100. ■ There might be insufficient acid. Taste the must, and if lacking in acid, add two teaspoons of citric acid/4.5 litres or adjust to pH 3.3. ■ Too much acid, check the pH – if it is below 3 the yeast may have been killed or inhibited. Adding a solution of potassium carbonate can solve this. ■ Not enough yeast nutrient has been added. Add some more. ■ The yeast might have been added too early and killed by the presence of Campden. Make up a new yeast culture and start again. ■ Are you sure you added the yeast?

Symptom	Possible causes	Reason and solutions

Frothing through the airlock

▦ Froth rising out of the fermenter airlock	▦ A vigorous fermentation ▦ Overfilling of fermenter	▦ There is no need for concern – apart from a bit of a mess – it is actually a good sign and indicates that the yeast is strong and fermenting vigorously. ▦ If overfilling is the cause, drain off some of the wine using a sterilised siphon. ▦ Clean and refill the airlock with water and allow the yeast to continue fermenting the wine. Frothing over can be avoided by using a larger fermenter.

Stuck fermentation

▦ The wine has not reached the expected final gravity (the gravity reading has not changed over a period of three or four days). ▦ This might be accompanied by no visible signs of continuing fermentation and no bubbles rising through the airlock.	▦ Poor ingredients (poorly fermentable must) ▦ Insufficient yeast nutrients ▦ Old yeast ▦ Temperature shock ▦ Fluctuating temperatures ▦ High alcohol levels ▦ Wrong strain of yeast	▦ Poor ingredients may result in a high proportion of complex carbohydrates relative to the proportion of simple carbohydrates (sugars) in the must. It is much easier for yeast to ferment simple sugars. High levels of complex carbohydrates will cause the fermentation to slow down considerably once the simple sugars have been used up. It may be possible for the yeast to ferment these but it can take a long time (several weeks). Hence, the fermentation may appear to become stuck. ▦ Insufficient nitrogen nutrients can cause yeast to stop working. This can occur with poor ingredients and with wines that are made using very high percentages of refined sugars such as ordinary household sugar. These sugars won't contain sufficient nutrients and will have a dilution effect on the nutrients provided by the other ingredients. For kits that require additional sugar, do not use more than is stated in the kit instructions. Stirring a yeast nutrient into the wine may help to rectify the problem. ▦ Temperature shock can cause yeast to stop working. If the temperature is allowed to become too high during the fermentation, it can kill the yeast. If it is allowed to become too low it will result in a very slow fermentation or no fermentation at all. ▦ The ideal fermentation temperature is 18° to 23°C. Rapid fluctuations, even within this range, can cause yeast to slow down or stop working. The temperature should be kept as constant as possible throughout the fermentation period. ▦ High alcohol levels inhibit and eventually kill yeast. Alcohol is a by-product of fermentation and the level gradually increases in the wine during fermentation. Different yeast strains can survive different levels of alcohol. ▦ It might not always be possible to re-start a stuck fermentation, but the following actions are often successful: ▦ Ensure the temperature of the wine is 18° to 23°C. Gently stir the wine to rouse the yeast, using a sterilised stirrer/spoon. This action alone will often start the yeast working again. ▦ Add a new sachet of yeast to the wine. This should first be rehydrated and activated by mixing the dried yeast into a glass of pre-boiled, lukewarm water together with a teaspoon of sugar. This should be covered and left in a warm place until seen to be actively fermenting, before adding it.

(Cath Harries)

Symptom	Possible causes	Reason and solutions
Wine is too acid		
Acid to taste	Created during fermentation	Reduce acidity of the wine by using a proprietary wine acid reduction solution or potassium carbonate solution.
Wine is too sweet		
Sweet to taste	Yeast not worked efficiently, or too much sugar at start.	Blend with a dry wine and use less sugar in the must next time.
Wine not clear		
Wine looks cloudy, hazy or foggy	Insufficient clearing time allowed Type of wine Excess complex carbohydrates in wine (poor ingredients) Contamination by wild yeasts or bacteria	When wine is bottled it is not unusual for it to display a degree of cloudiness caused by yeast cells in suspension. Clearing usually takes around two weeks, but can vary significantly – so be patient. Moving the wine to a cooler place can help. A wine that doesn't clear is still likely to be drinkable in many cases. Taste it and see. If the wine contains excessive amounts of complex carbohydrates and proteins it may not clear completely. This is usually a result of poor quality ingredients, but it may still be drinkable. The use of a fining agent (available from home winemaker suppliers) can be used to aid clearing in many cases. Follow the instructions supplied. If the wine is contaminated by wild yeasts or bacteria it is unlikely to clear. It may also be undrinkable (see section: **Spoiled/infected wine**)
Pectin haze		
Hazy wine	Test for pectin haze: Add four parts of methylated spirit to one part of wine, mixing and leaving for thirty minutes. The formation of clots, strings or jelly indicates pectin in the wine.	Add a liquid pectic enzyme and leave until clear. Siphon off the sediment if necessary.

Symptom	Possible causes	Reason and solutions
Starch haze		
Hazy wine	Test by adding a drop of brown iodine solution to a small volume of wine. A blue-black colour indicates starch.	Add fungal amylase or diastase and leave until clear.
Spoiled/infected wine		
Sour acid taste and an oily, thick or slimy appearance Unusual taste and smell (vinegar, sour, wet cardboard, mouldy, musty, straw, TCP) Wine cloudy – although this isn't always a sign of infection (see section: **Wine not clear**) A ring of scum on the inside neck of wine bottles, near the wine line. Mould on surface of must	Lactic acid bacteria, throw it away Contamination by bacteria, wild yeasts or mould spores from inadequately cleaned and sterilised brewing equipment, or from the air.	Cleanliness is essential... It is the home winemaker's challenge to prevent contamination by spoilage organisms. A comprehensive cleaning and sanitising regime will reduce the number of potential spoilage organisms to a minimum but never eradicate them completely. It is essential that all equipment that comes into contact with the wine is thoroughly cleaned and sterilised before use. Various sterilising and cleaning agents are available from home winemaker suppliers and the instructions should be carefully followed. Scouring pads, stiff brushes should not be used to clean equipment, particularly the fermenter. This is because such items will leave minute scratches on the walls which create an ideal place for bacteria to harbour, thereby increasing the chances of the wine becoming infected. The inside of the fermenter should only be cleaned with a soft cloth, and any caked-on residues soaked off rather than scrubbed. Once the wine has been mixed (concentrate/sugar/water) there should not be any delay in adding the yeast. The faster the yeast starts to work, the less chance of contamination (because the yeast will compete against potential spoilage organisms). Often winemakers use too much hot water and then wait for the must temperature to fall before pitching the yeast. This is a critical time for potential spoilage organisms to get a foothold – the longer the delay, the more likely the wine will become infected. It is far better to get the temperature correct to start with, which should be around 18° to 23°C. Follow the wine kit instructions carefully. Avoid exposing the wine to the air. Ensure the lid is put on to the fermenter as soon as the ingredients have been dissolved and the yeast has been added. It should only be necessary to remove the lid and expose the wine when taking hydrometer readings and during bottling. Keep windows closed when winemaking. Do not leave the wine for overly extended periods in the fermenter. Despite a high standard of hygiene it is still possible to experience a bad wine. This is because there will always be airborne bacteria and wild yeasts present when preparing, fermenting and bottling. It's just bad luck. It isn't possible to save a bad wine, so discard it. Clean and sterilise the equipment thoroughly and start again.
Exploding wine bottles		
Corks pop out of wine bottles Wine gushing when bottles are opened	Wine bottled too early Poor sterilisation of bottles Overfilling of bottles	Always check the wine with a hydrometer to ensure fermentation is complete prior to bottling. Fermentation can begin again if the wine was not allowed to ferment to dryness. Poor sterilisation of the bottles may allow the wine to come into contact with wild yeast, which can result in carbonation (fizziness) and possibly off flavours. Ensure the bottles are thoroughly sterilised. Then thoroughly rinse with cold tap water before filling with wine. Bottles should be filled to allow 15mm of head space. Change the stopper on the bottle – plastic stoppers with a valve in are available. An old fashioned remedy was to pour out some of the wine and replace with a glass of brandy or other spirits. This should kill off the yeast. Pour the wine into a fermenting vessel and let the fermentation finish. Add a stabiliser to kill the wine off. Beware the addition of too many Campden tablets as they will taint the wine.
Sediment		
A narrow layer of sediment at the bottom of the bottles.	Yeast sediment	It's perfectly normal. The sediment is the result of the yeast settling out of suspension after the secondary fermentation has finished. A thick layer of sediment may indicate that the wine was bottled too early. It may also be the result of accidentally siphoning over some of the sediment from the bottom of the fermenter. Care should be taken to avoid siphoning any of the sediment from the fermenter during the bottling. Leaving wine on a thick layer of sediment can result in off flavours developing during storage (see section: **Unusual taste**).

Symptom	Possible causes	Reason and solutions
Unusual taste		
■ The wine has an unusual taste and/or smell. ■ Medicinal flavour ■ Bad-egg smell ■ Acetic or vinegar flavours	■ Spoiled/infected wine ■ Infection ■ Lack of acid in the must ■ Yeast may have been added to the sulphited must too soon ■ Bacterial infection	■ A very wide range of unusual (and unpleasant) flavours can be caused by spoilage from bacteria, moulds and wild yeasts (see section: **Spoiled/infected wine**). ■ Throw away the wine and sterilize all equipment. ■ High fermentation temperatures and fluctuations in temperature can cause off-flavours to be produced (fruity, solvent). Ensure fermentation is carried out at the correct temperature (18° to 23°C) and avoid fluctuations. ■ Yeast breakdown can result in off flavours (eg rotten vegetables, meaty, marmite). This is a common result of leaving the wine in the fermenter for too long, sitting on that layer of dead yeast. ■ Throw away the wine and include more acid in the next batch. ■ The addition of one Campden tablet per five litres may solve the problem. If not, dispose of the wine. Note that a very dry wine can have apple acetic flavours, not caused by infection. The addition of sugar will solve this.
Wine smells or tastes of sherry (unintentionally)		
■ Sherry flavours, leather, straw	■ Caused by acetaldehyde formation due to presence of air	■ Try dissolving one or two Campden tablets per 5 litres. Ensure all storage vessels are kept topped up to minimise contact with air.
Wine lacks nose or bouquet		
■ Wine has no aroma	■ Lack of acid in the must	■ The addition of lactic acid to the wine and a longer maturation may solve the problem.
Wine lacks body		
■ Lack of balance, poor mouthfeel, little perception of fruit on the palate, thinness, watery feel	■ Not enough fruit in the must	■ Add some concentrated grape juice. This will also sweeten the wine.

(Cath Harries)

Symptom	Possible causes	Reason and solutions
'Geranium' character		
▨ A strong resemblance to geranium leaves in aroma and flavour.	▨ Malolactic bacteria acting on potassium sorbate	▨ No easy treatment
Wine tastes flat, insipid		
▨ Poor mouthfeel, no sparkle or life	▨ Not enough tannin or acid	▨ Add a little tannin to taste
Astringency		
▨ Mouth puckering taste	▨ Excessive tannins	▨ Excess tannin can be removed by fining with isinglass or a longer maturation.
Bitterness		
▨ Sour or bitter taste	▨ An excess of sour ingredients in the must, such as citrus pith.	▨ The addition of a small amount of glycerol may mask it.

Winemaker's Log

Inoculation

Date / Time: _____

Varietal: _____

Kit / Source: _____

Yeast: _____

Additional Notes:

_____

_____

_____

Must Temperature: _____

Specific Gravity: _____

pH: _____ TA: _____

First Racking

Date / Time: _____

pH: _____ TA: _____

Additional Notes:

_____

_____

_____

Wine Temperature: _____

Specific Gravity: _____

Stabilizing & Clarifying

Date / Time: _____

pH: _____ TA: _____

Additional Notes:

_____

_____

_____

Wine Temperature: _____

Specific Gravity: _____

Bottling

Date / Time: _____

Additional Notes:

_____

_____

Wine Temperature: _____

Keeping a winemaking log

The better the records you keep the better the wine you will make.

It is important to keep records on the ingredients and quantities used, temperatures, times and even your perceptions of the outcomes.

There are several winemaking spreadsheets and apps available over the internet that can be a big help. However, some of the spreadsheets can be complicated – a simple pen and notebook still proves to be ideal for most people. As soon as you open a notebook, it is ready to use and shut it up and it immediately closes down without fear of losing any data.

And should you have the misfortune to pour sugar solution over it – it will get wet and sticky but most of the contents will be retrievable. A similar incident with an electronic notebook could be terminal.

Keeping a log is important as it allows you the opportunity to try and recreate your better vintages and not repeat those you were dissatisfied with.

A good start is to write up each recipe in a consistent, simple manner. Just put down what you did and when you did it.

It is important to write everything down. Then if you are trying to troubleshoot and retrace your steps you have a good record of what you did. And the opposite is true too – in the years to come you might open a bottle of wine and find it is near perfect. If you knew how it was made, you might be able to recreate it.

WHAT TO PUT INTO THE LOG

- Record the how, what, when and why.
- Record where the raw materials came from and what their condition is.
- The date and time is important.
- Air temperature.
- Must temperature.
- Must colour.
- Airlock activity level.
- Smell.
- Taste of the must.
- Specific gravity.
- Additives and other processing aids added, and why.
- Acidity of the must/pH.
- Titratable acidity.
- Record any interaction with the wine such as stirring or what you did if the fermentation became stuck.
- Good record keeping is invaluable. Besides the original winemaking process, if you blend your wines, keep a record of the quantities used. That way you'll have a chance of repeating a good result, or avoiding a bad one.

(Cath Harries)

A home winemaker's calendar

What to make and when? There's always a wine to keep your fermenters busy, even if you do not want to make your wine from grapes. You don't have to wait until harvest time to make country wine. The ingredients might be in your home, garden, hedgerow or freezer. And if all else fails, just head off to the supermarket. Recipes for these wines can be found online.

January
- Figs, dates, raisins, prunes or other dried fruits
- Barley
- Oranges or other citrus fruits

February
- Parsnips will be in the supermarkets, or you might have them on your allotment
- Go nutty, try almonds or walnut

March
- Go bananas, they can make an interesting wine
- Rice and sultanas
- Canned fruits – such as peaches or pineapple

April
- The hedgerows (and maybe your lawn) are probably bursting with a yellow carpet of dandelion flowers
- Gorse
- Primrose

May
- The hedgerows should be full of blossom
- Elderflower makes the best sparkling country wine
- Nettle is an old English favourite

▼ **Elderflower picked from the hedgerow makes a delicious sparkling wine.** (Tim Hampson)

▶ **Nettles might be tricky to pick, but they make a refreshing and surprisingly good wine.**
(Tim Hampson)

June

- Red and blackcurrant bushes should be fruiting
- Nettles
- Gooseberries
- Consider herbs – parsley, rosemary or sage

July

- Cherries
- Flowers: honeysuckle, marigold
- Marrows and courgettes
- Strawberry

August

- Raspberry
- Plum
- Rose petals
- Carrots

September

- Rosehip
- Rosemary
- Apples and pears
- Soft fruits

October

- It's a berry good time – seek out hawthornberry, bilberry or mulberry
- Potatoes

November

- Sloe gin
- Port
- Parsnips
- Celery

December

- Get spicy, ginger, spiced beetroot
- Mulled wine

▶ **Rosemary is one of the many herbs growing in most gardens which can be an interesting ingredient in wines.** (Tim Hampson)

(Cath Harries)

Some useful contacts

If you have a problem with your winemaking, help is never far away.

Brew Shop

Excellent supplier of winemaking equipment and ingredients, based in Stockport, Cheshire.
www.thebrewshop.com

Brew UK

Specialist supplier of home brew ingredients and equipment
www.brewuk.co.uk

Home Brew Shop

One of the best known suppliers of home brew equipment and ingredients.
www.the-home-brew-shop.co.uk

National Association of Wine and Beermakers

An organisation that draws together individuals, clubs, and federations in England who are involved in wine and beer making at home. It organises an annual conference and exhibition.
www.nawb.org.uk

(Cath Harries)

GLOSSARY

Acetic acid – Caused by a bacterium present in most wines, if it is in excess then it turns it to vinegar.

Acids – The compounds which give wine its crisp taste. The four major acids are tartaric, malic, lactic and citric and are found in all grapes. Acidity is an essential component of wine. It helps red wines keep their colour and gives white wines their balance. Too much acidity, and a wine is tart and unpleasant; too little and the wine is flabby and uninteresting.

Aeration – The process of incorporating air into a wine or juice, usually through splashing while racking, or simply by stirring a container very vigorously. This is sometimes done to remove undesirable aromas such as hydrogen sulphide, or to give an initial dose of oxygen to a fermentation just getting under way.

Aerobic fermentation – A fermentation conducted in the presence of fresh air. Aerobic conditions are necessary for yeast to rapidly reproduce to a density conducive to the fast production of alcohol.

Ageing – Many wines improve with age, and trying older wines is one of life's joys. How wine ages is complex and has much to do with the conditions the wine is kept in.

(Winzer Sommerach)

(Wines of Argentina)

Airlock – A simple plastic or glass device used during fermentation to keep airborne contamination away from the fermentation jar whilst still allowing carbon dioxide to escape.

Alcohol – Commonly used term for ethyl alcohol or ethanol. It is a by-product of the fermentation of sugars by yeast.

Amylase – An enzyme that converts starch to fermentable compounds.

Anaerobic fermentation – A fermentation conducted in the absence of fresh air, as in a fermentation vat or demijohn fitted with an airlock.

Anthocyanins – The pigments in grapes that contribute the red and purple colours in wine.

Antioxidant – A compound which retards oxidation and slows its effects in wine. Sulphur dioxide is the most widely used winemaking antioxidant. It also serves as an antimicrobial agent.

Aroma – The smell or bouquet of a wine.

Ascorbic acid – Commonly known as Vitamin C, it is used to stop the oxidation of wine.

Astringency – A taste and a mouthfeel that's tongue puckering – not easy to describe, but you know it when you taste it.

Autolysis – The breakdown of dead yeast cells in a wine, giving a rich flavour, structure and body to wines like Champagne, and those made from Chardonnay or Sauvignon Blanc.

Balance – A wine is balanced when it has all the ingredients present in the correct proportion. It's hard to define, but you know it when the component parts – acid, fruit, tannin, sugar and alcohol – are chorusing in harmony.

Barrique – A small oak barrel (normally 225 litres) of the type originally found in Bordeaux, but now used worldwide.

Bentonite – A fining agent made of clay particles which helps clear cloudy wine.

Bite – The astringency of a wine, produced by tannin. Without sufficient tannin, a wine may taste dull and lifeless.

Blending – The process of mixing different wines. Classic Bordeaux, for example, is a blend of Cabernet Sauvignon, Cabernet Franc and Merlot.

Bodega – A Spanish wine cellar; also refers to a seller of an alcoholic beverage.

Body – The viscosity or fullness of a wine.

Bouquet – The smell or aroma of a wine.

Brilliance – A term used to describe the clarity of a wine.

Brix – Usually thought of as a sweetness scale, Brix measures the amount of sugar in the original grape juice.

Buttery – Taste term for the rich, creamy characters often found in barrel-fermented Chardonnay that has undergone malolactic fermentation.

Calcium carbonate – Also known as precipitated chalk.

Campden tablets – Used as a preservative or for sterilising ingredients and equipment before use. Their use also prevents oxidation and the growth of bacteria, fungi and moulds.

Cantina – Italian term for winery.

Cap – Fruit skins, stems and pulp that float to the surface during a fermentation. It is essential to punch down the cap into the wine during a red wine fermentation to extract valuable tannins and coloured compounds.

Carbon dioxide (CO$_2$) – A gas created during fermentation as the yeast converts the sugar into alcohol.

Cava – Spanish sparkling wine made using the traditional Champagne method.

Chaptalise – To add sugar to grape juice that does not naturally have enough sugar to make a decent wine.

Claret – English term for red wines from the Bordeaux region of France.

Cold stabilisation – In essence, chilling a wine solely to precipitate out the natural potassium bitartrate crystals, to ease wine buyers' fears that it is unnatural.

Country wine – A non-grape wine. Can be made from fruit, vegetables, flowers or cereals.

Cuvée – A winemaking term relating to the specially blended base white wine that will be made to undergo a secondary fermentation in the production of sparkling wines. It also refers to a blend of different wines.

Débourbage – The process in which the must of a white wine is allowed to settle before racking off the wine; this reduces the need for filtration or fining.

Demijohn – A glass, sometimes plastic, 4.5 litre fermentation jar; in the US it is often referred to as a carboy.

Demi-sec – French for medium dry.

Diastase – The enzyme which converts starch to sugar and thus prevents starch haze in a finished wine. Also known as fungal amylase.

Dry – The taste of a wine which has no remaining sugar and no hint of sweetness.

Eiswein – German for ice wine, a dessert wine made from frozen grapes.

Energisers – Energisers are yeast nutrients usually with Vitamin B1 added and are used to speed up a slow or stuck fermentation.

Enzyme – A chemical compound which can convert complex molecules, such as starch, to simpler ones such as sugar. Enzymes produced by yeast cells convert sugar into alcohol during fermentation.

Epsom salts – Also known as magnesium sulphate, it can be used as a yeast nutrient.

Extended maceration – Letting red grapes sit for a while before being pressed, so that flavour and richness develop.

Fermentation – The process whereby yeast as part of its lifecycle converts sugar into carbon dioxide and creates the 'waste product' alcohol.

Filtering – The process of removing haze from wine. It makes the wine stable and it is less likely to re-ferment in the bottle.

Finings – Substances used to clear wine. Haze particles attach themselves to them and sink to the bottom of the container as sediment. The most common finings are derived from isinglass, gelatine, chitin or bentonite.

Fino – A dry, light style of sherry.

Flor – A growth of yeast cells formed on the surface of a wine during the making of sherry.

Fortification – The addition of alcohol, usually a distilled spirit, to a finished wine to increase its alcoholic strength. Port and sherry are the two best known fortified wines.

Fructose – A simple sugar, one of the constituents of sucrose.

Glucose – One of the two sugars (the other is fructose) formed when ordinary sugar (sucrose) is broken down by yeast enzyme action.

Glycerol/Glycerine – An additive used to mask harshness or immaturity in rough wine.

Haze – A cloudy appearance in wine.

Hydrometer – An instrument used to measure the specific gravity/sugar content of a wine at different stages of production from start to finish.

Infection – A wine is said to be infected when it is contaminated by an unwanted organism.

Isinglass – A fining, it is derived from the air or swim bladders of freshwater fish.

Lees – The sediment at the bottom of a fermentation vessel. It is made up of dead yeast cells and other proteins.

Liqueur – A strong alcoholic drink made from distilled spirits, with additional flavouring added such as herbs and spices.

Maceration – The process of leaving grape juice in contact with the skins and seeds.

Malic acid – A component of grapes, it contributes a pleasant sourness. It encourages fermentation and produces aroma and flavour. It is found in high concentrations in unripe grapes and has a tart, sharp flavour. It is lost as the grapes ripen. Malic acid is low in wines grown in warm regions.

Malolactic fermentation – The conversion of malic acid into the softer, less harsh lactic acid by lactic acid bacteria. It takes place after alcoholic fermentation.

Marc – Another term for *pomace*. Also, a spirit made from it by distillation.

Maturation – After fermentation, wine needs to mature before it is ready to drink.

Metabisulphite – Sodium and potassium metabisulphite are sterilising agents – sometimes known as Campden tablets. They are used to sterilise ingredients, equipment and (when racking) to inhibit yeast growth and reduce oxidation.

Must – grape liquid before it has been converted to wine by fermentation.

Nose – The smell, aroma or bouquet of a wine. Winemakers also nose a wine – it's a posh way of saying they smell it.

Nutrients – Chemical compounds such as ammonium

(Cath Harries)

sulphate, phosphate and vitamin B, which encourage the growth of yeast.

Oak chippings – Used to flavour red wine to give it an aroma, as if the wine has been stored in oak barrels.

Oenology – The science of winemaking.

Oenophile – A wine aficionado or connoisseur. Some are professionals, many are amateurs, but they appreciate and often collect wine, particularly grape wines from certain regions, varietal types, or methods.

Off flavour – A taste that destroys the true flavour of a wine, it is usually due to bacteria or a poor fermentation.

Oxidation – the process by which alcohol is converted to aldehyde compounds, thus spoiling the wine's taste, look and smell. However, carefully controlled oxidation can be used to produce sherry.

pH – A measure of a liquid's acidity. A wine with a pH of 3 is 10 times more acidic than a wine with a pH of 4. The higher the pH, the lower the acidity, and the lower the pH, the higher the acidity.

Phylloxera – A very nasty bug, akin to an aphid, that just about wiped out the vineyards in Europe in the second half of the last century.

Pigeage – The skins of the red grapes form a 'cap' on top of the wine when it ferments. This cap must be broken up and stirred back into the wine. This breaking up is called pigeage.

Pomace – What is left behind when the must is pressed, and the juice is all removed.

Port – A sweet fortified wine, which is produced from grapes grown and processed in the Douro region of Portugal. This wine is fortified with the addition of distilled grape spirits in order to boost the alcohol content and stop fermentation, thus preserving some of the natural grape sugars.

Premier cru – French term for a first growth, it is used mostly in conjunction with the wines of Burgundy and Champagne.

Primary fermentation – The main fermentation that turns a vat of grape juice into a wine. This is where the yeast works on the sugars in the raw juice, converting those sugars to alcohol and carbon dioxide.

Punch down – The pushing down of the fruit and stalks during the primary fermentation. This process aids the incorporation of oxygen to the yeasts and slows the rate of oxidation of the fruit.

Punt – The indentation found in the base of a wine bottle. According to some wine experts the punt depth is thought to be related to wine quality, with better quality wines having a deeper punt.

Racking – The process of siphoning wine from one container to another. It is typically used to describe the process of filling bottles.

Re-fermentation – The process of a wine fermenting for a second time; also called secondary fermentation. It is usually caused by the addition of sugar to sweeten the wine or a sudden warm spell. Using potassium sorbate and a Campden tablet will terminate any yeast activity.

Rosé – A wine that is pale pink to light red in colour.

Sec – French term for dry, as in the opposite of sweet.

Sediment – The debris that accumulates at the bottom of a vessel during fermentation or maturation. Predominantly dead yeast cells, it is also known as lees.

Sherry – A fortified wine that has been subjected to controlled oxidation to produce a distinctive flavour.

Siphon – A long plastic tube used for racking and bottling the wine.

Solera – The Spanish system of mixing wines of different ages which is often used for fortified wines. One-quarter to one-third of the oldest wine is drawn off for bottling and replaced with the next oldest wine, which in turn is replaced with the next-yet oldest wine, and so on until the youngest wine is being used to replace the next-youngest.

Specific gravity (SG) – The density of a liquid. Pure water has a specific gravity of 1.000. As the amount of sugar in a liquid increases, the specific gravity (SG) goes up. By using a hydrometer and measuring the SG at the start and end of fermentation, the amount of alcohol can be determined.

Spumante – Italian for sparkling.

Stuck fermentation – A fermentation that has started but then stops before converting all fermentable sugar. Usually due to an imbalance in the ingredients, or to temperature extremes unacceptable to the yeast.

Sucrose – The chemical name for ordinary household sugar. It is composed of glucose and fructose molecules combined to form a complex sugar.

Sulphite (also sulfite) – Sulphur compound added to a wine to kill off the wild yeasts, so that a known yeast can be added to the wine.

Sur lie – French for leaving wine on the lees. This is the process of leaving the lees in the wine for a few months to a year, accompanied by a regime of periodic stirring. It can add complexity to a wine.

Tannin – An astringent substance which is an important ingredient of many wines, providing a vital element of the overall flavour. Tannins actually denature (change the structure of) the salivary proteins, causing a rough sandpapery feel in the mouth.

Tartaric acid – The main acid present in ripe grapes. It plays a vital part in the maturing of wines.

Tartrate crystals – White crystals that fall to the bottom of a vessel, they are a natural part of winemaking.

Ullage – The air space between the top of the wine in a container and the cap or cork.

Varietal – A wine named after the single grape variety it was made from.

Vinometer – An instrument used for the measuring of alcohol content in wines.

Vitamin C – The common name for ascorbic acid. It is an antioxidant which helps to preserve wine.

Yeast – A living single celled micro-organism, once known as 'god is good'. By feeding off fermentable sugars it creates carbon dioxide and alcohol. Most yeasts suitable for winemaking die when the alcoholic strength reaches about 16 per cent ABV.

Yeast starter – The process of kick-starting yeast into life before adding it to the must. When making wine at home, a common way to start dried yeast is to put some into a cup containing a half teaspoon of sugar and some warm water.

Zymase – The enzymes produced by yeast which convert glucose and fructose into alcohol.

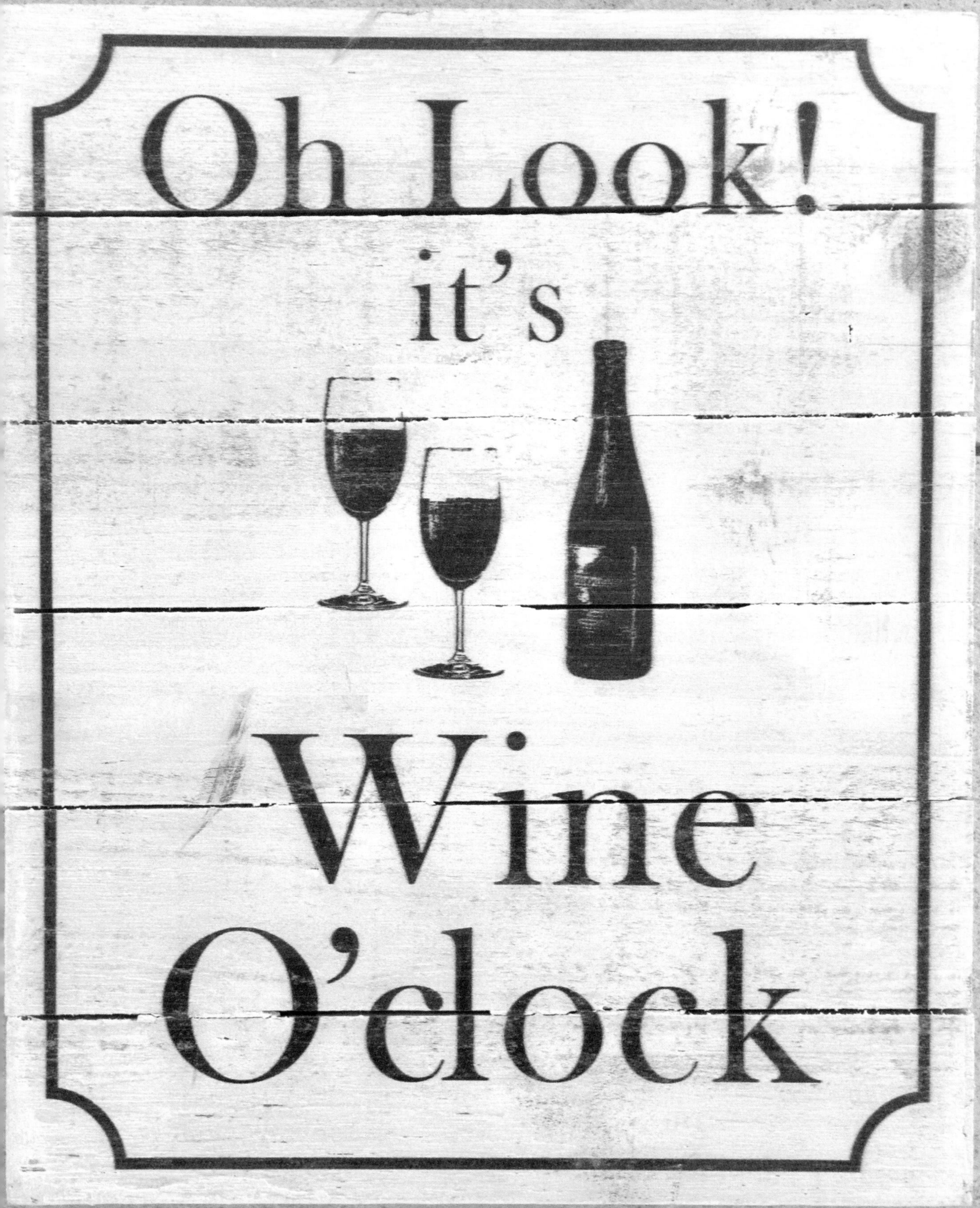
Oh Look!
it's
Wine
O'clock